MADHUR JAFFREY'S
Instantly Indian Cookbook

MADHUR JAFFREY'S
Instantly Indian Cookbook

Photographs by Dana Gallagher

ALFRED A. KNOPF   NEW YORK   2019

THIS IS A BORZOI BOOK
PUBLISHED BY ALFRED A. KNOPF

www.aaknopf.com

Knopf, Borzoi Books, and the colophon are registered trademarks
of Penguin Random House LLC.

Library of Congress Cataloging-in-Publication Data
Names: Jaffrey, Madhur, [date] author.
Title: Madhur Jaffrey's instantly Indian cookbook / Madhur Jaffrey.
Description: First edition. | New York : Alfred A. Knopf, 2019. | Includes index.
Identifiers: LCCN 2018040124 | ISBN 9780525655794 (hardcover : alk. paper)
Subjects: LCSH: Cooking, Indic. | Pressure cooking. | LCGFT: Cookbooks.
Classification: LCC TX724.5.I4 J2728 2019 | DDC 641.59/297—dc23 LC record available
at https://lccn.loc.gov/2018040124

Instant Pot® is a registered trademark of Instant Brands, Inc.
The author and publisher of this book are not affiliated with Instant Brands, Inc.,
the maker of the Instant Pot®, nor is this book authorized, licensed, or endorsed by Instant Brands, Inc.

Case photograph by Dana Gallagher
Case design by Kelly Blair

Manufactured in Canada
First Edition

THIS BOOK IS DEDICATED TO MY FAMILY

Sanford

Zia

Sakina and Frank

Meera and Craig

Robi

Cassius

and

Jamila

I love them all so much

Contents

Introduction

The idea of traditional Indian food being prepared with the help of a pressure cooker is not new or alien to me or to any Indian. For at least the last forty years, almost every middle-class Indian household has had one, two, or even three pressure cookers whistling away in their kitchens to let them know that their dried split peas are done or their rice is ready or that their meat is tender.

I was drawn to the Instant Pot because it was not only a pressure cooker that allowed me to cook fast but much, much more. It could work as a slow cooker too, braising meats to a lovely tenderness in five to ten hours; it could transform itself into a rice cooker, cooking rice to perfection without any outside guidance; it could make my soups and stocks; and it could pressure steam as well, cooking a dozen or more hard-boiled eggs so beautifully that their shells slipped off with ease and allowed me to drop them into my curry sauces without a care in the world.

Having said all this, I have to stress that the Instant Pot is not a Magic Pot. It will not, in most cases, take over and cook for you (though sometimes it can). It is a multipurpose cooking utensil that takes some experimentation to master. If you want your fish to be just done and not overcooked, if you want your vegetables tender-crisp, if you want your meat to be tender but not dry and rigid, if you want to cook your dried beans evenly, then give the pot some time and patience. Work with it. Play with it. The pot allows for many possibilities, many combinations and permutations of its functions. Take the time and examine what they are.

To begin with, read the booklet that comes with the Instant Pot. This way you will understand its basic functions and its many dos and don'ts. After that, allow your own palate to tell you what you like and don't like. For example, generally I do not like my fish cooked under pressure at all. I prefer making the sauce first and then slipping the fish into the sauce and poaching it briefly using the Sauté function. I also found that I preferred chicken cooked under Low Pressure rather than High Pressure. These are things that I learned as I cooked and experimented.

Also know that even though you are cooking in an Instant Pot, it takes time for it to come up to pressure. It is hard to predict just how much time this might be. It depends upon the amount of liquid and solids in the pot. Similarly, it takes time for the pressure to drop, time you may not have allowed for but should.

Once you understand this, the Instant Pot becomes the friend you always wanted in the kitchen. Now that I have it, I would not want to be without it. It cooks my dried beans and split peas (what Indians call dals) to perfection as it does my basmati rice. I love how my cauliflower turns out and I adore my Instant Pot egg curries. I also love my soups. Especially my Mulligatawny soup.

I have tested all the dishes in this book in the IP-DUO60 V3, 6-quart Instant Pot. You might want to make slight changes to your recipes according to which particular pot you own.

RICE When I acquired my Instant Pot, I knew that I could handle the pressure-cooking part. What I have gotten to know and love are the other special functions. The RICE function works perfectly. Just follow my directions for measuring and soaking the rice, then press RICE and let the machine do the rest. Even those of you who have been afraid of cooking rice will be left speechless. Just remember that you can ruin the delicate grains of rice when you serve them. Rice grains clump up. To separate them, slide the paddle provided with the machine down one side of the pot all the way to the bottom, then turn the paddle so it is parallel with the bottom of the inner pot and remove a lump of rice. Press down on the lump gently with the flat side of the paddle. The rice grains will fall apart naturally and easily.

If you are using basmati rice, always get the best-quality Indian basmati from an Indian grocer. Just ask the grocer, "What is your best-quality basmati rice?" It is often slightly yellowed, as it has been aged for at least six months. It will also be the most expensive.

CHICKEN When I cook chicken parts in my Instant Pot, I find that their texture is best if I cook them under **LOW PRESSURE** for six minutes and then use the **SAUTÉ** function to cook them gently for another seven to ten minutes. Don't be afraid to experiment with any of the functions to make your food turn out just the way you want it.

MEAT Meat may be cooked at **HIGH PRESSURE**, but it is at its tender best when cooked using the **SLOW COOK** button. Shoulder of lamb, which I use in many recipes, will take about five hours to cook, but this is painless time that leaves you free to do other things.

BOILED EGGS I find that hard-boiled eggs turn out perfectly using the **STEAM** button. The shells slip off easily so you do not have to worry even when using very fresh eggs. Also, you can boil up a large number of eggs at the same time, which is particularly useful when making an egg curry. (For more on cooking these eggs, see Pressure-Cooked Eggs, page 74.)

FISH On the whole, fish is very delicate for pressure cooking. So, what I do is make the sauce I want using the pressure cooker but then I turn to the **SAUTÉ** function and poach the fish pieces in the sauce. This works for fish filets and shrimp. For clams, I make the sauce using pressure, then I turn on the **SAUTÉ** function, cover the pot with the glass lid (see below), and let the clams steam open.

This leads me to what extra parts you should buy to complement those that come with the Instant Pot. I find the steaming basket, the glass lid, and an extra inner pot to be absolute essentials. Not much else is needed.

If you wish to steam something in a bowl, you will find a sling to lower and raise the bowl out of the hot water to be very useful. It is easy to make it at home. Take two feet of heavy-duty aluminum foil and spread it out on a flat surface in front of you. Lift the side closest to you and fold it up one-third of the way, then press down on the fold. Now fold the top section over the bottom folded area and press down on the fold once again to flatten your sling. Fold the ends of the sling over the bowl when you do your steaming.

Many of the recipes have more ingredients than you may be used to using. Do not let that worry you. I did not want to dumb down India's authentic tastes for this book. Remember that Indian food is as great as it is because of its magical use of spices, which offers both a variety of changing flavors and aromas as well as medicinal properties that heal and prevent disease. Turmeric, for example, is a serious antiseptic. Many Americans today put it in their teas and drinks. Well, Indians use it daily in the food we cook. Also, remember that if you are putting in one spice, you can just as easily put in four or eight. To make it easier for yourself, read the recipe carefully first. Chop and cut whatever you need before you start cooking. If four spices or other ingredients go into the pot at the same time, collect them in small or large bowls as needed. Arrange the ingredients in the order in which they go into the pot. After that, the cooking will be a breeze.

Indian dishes often need chutneys and little salads and yogurt relishes to complete them. Many of these are not cooked and do not require an Instant Pot. But my book requires that they be available to you. So you will find them in a special chapter, "Side Dishes."

Not all the Indian food in this book has to be eaten as part of a large Indian meal. For example, the Black-eyed Peas with Mushrooms (page 27) may be put into a bowl topped with some Cucumber, Tomato, and Onion Salad (page 137) and just eaten with a spoon. Some crusty bread on the side wouldn't hurt.

When we were children in India, my mother would leave lunch leftovers for us in the oven. When we came home from school, we would cut off thick ends from loaves of bread, hollow them out, and fill them with, say, Ground Lamb with Peas (page 98), topped with pickles or yogurt salads, and then just devour them. In a similar spirit, you can make sloppy joes with some of the meat dishes.

Feel easy with the recipes and incorporate them into your lives in ways that best suit you. The foods in this book are very Indian. But you may eat them in as American a way as you like.

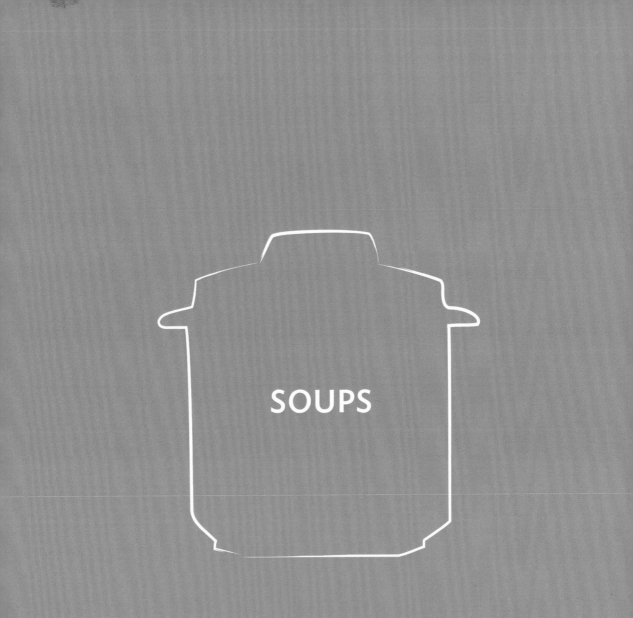

SOUPS

COLD YOGURT SOUP WITH CHICKPEAS, CUCUMBERS, AND TOMATOES

Dahi Aur Chanay Ka Soup

SERVES 4

A lovely cooling soup.

2 cups plain yogurt

1 cup chickpea broth (see
Plain Chickpeas, page 20)

2 cups strained chicken broth

1 cup peeled and finely diced
tomatoes

1 cup peeled and finely diced
cucumbers

½ teaspoon salt (more if the
chicken broth is unsalted)

Freshly ground black pepper

¼ teaspoon chili powder

½ teaspoon ground roasted
cumin seeds (page 152)

1 cup cooked chickpeas (see
Plain Chickpeas, page 20)

Cilantro or mint leaves,
chopped, for garnishing

Put the yogurt in a bowl. Beat with a fork or whisk until smooth and creamy. Add the chickpea broth and the chicken broth. Stir to mix. Now add all the remaining ingredients except the cilantro or mint. Mix gently. Keep covered and refrigerated. Serve garnished with the cilantro or mint.

CREAMY CAULIFLOWER SOUP

MAKES ABOUT 7½ CUPS AND SERVES 4–6

This rather unctuous soup is flavored with ginger. I serve it both hot and cold—garnished with a few chopped-up cilantro leaves, if hot, or finely cut chives, if cold. If you are serving it hot, do offer some Croutons (page 148) with it, along with some extra wedges of lemon.

3 tablespoons peanut or olive oil

1 medium onion, chopped

One 1-inch piece peeled fresh ginger, very finely chopped

2 cloves garlic, peeled and finely chopped

2 teaspoons ground cumin

2 teaspoons ground coriander

¼ teaspoon ground turmeric

⅛–¼ teaspoon chili powder

2 medium red potatoes (about 8–9 ounces), peeled and chopped

8–9 ounces (about 2 heaping cups) chopped cauliflower florets

5 cups chicken or vegetable stock

Salt as needed (this will depend on how salted your stock is), starting with ½ teaspoon

1 tablespoon lemon juice, or more as desired

¾ cup heavy cream

Cilantro sprigs or chives and Croutons (page 148) if desired, for garnishing

1. Select the SAUTÉ setting on your Instant Pot and set to More. When the display reads Hot, add oil, put in the onions. Stir and sauté for 2 minutes. Add the ginger and garlic. Stir and cook another 2 minutes. Add the cumin, coriander, turmeric, and chili powder. Stir once and add the potatoes, cauliflower, stock, and salt. Hit CANCEL to stop the cooking process.

2. Close and seal the lid. Cook on LOW PRESSURE for 5 minutes, releasing the steam manually after that. Hit CANCEL again. Open the lid carefully, venting the steam away from you. Wearing oven mitts, lift the inner pot out of the outer pot and let the soup cool. Blend it thoroughly in batches, straining each batch through a coarse strainer. Add the lemon juice and cream. Stir to mix, and taste for balance of flavors.

3. Serve hot or cold with the cilantro or chives, and croutons, if desired.

MY MOTHER'S RED LENTIL SOUP

SERVES 4

This soup, with just a hint of cloves, is very mild and simple yet so very satisfying and delicious. We often had it as a first course as children, and I make it for my family and friends all the time. It has become our soul food. You may serve it with Croutons (page 000) if you like, but they are not essential. What *are* essential are the lime or lemon juice and the cilantro.

All cooked split peas and beans tend to thicken as they sit. Thin the soup down to the consistency you like. I often end up adding up to a cup of water when I reheat it.

If you are feeding children, you can leave out the chili powder, just as my mother did when I was little.

1 cup split red lentils, washed in several changes of water and drained

¼ teaspoon ground turmeric

⅛ teaspoon clove powder

⅛ teaspoon chili powder (more for those who want it)

¾ teaspoon salt

A little finely chopped cilantro leaves

Lime or lemon wedges, for squeezing over the top

1. Put the washed and drained lentils, 3½ cups water, turmeric, clove powder, chili powder, and salt into the inner container of the Instant Pot. Close and seal the lid. Select the **PRESSURE COOK** function, set to low pressure, and cook for 5 minutes. Release the pressure manually. Open the lid carefully, venting the steam facing away from you. Stir the soup, mashing the lentils against the sides of the pot as you do so. Taste for balance of flavors and check the consistency. Thin the soup out with hot water to the thickness you like. Serve garnished with the cilantro and offer the lime or lemon wedges for squeezing on as much juice as desired.

GUJARATI MANGO SOUP

SERVES 6

This recipe, which I got from a South African Gujarati family, is not really a soup but rather a sweet and sour soupy dish called *fajeto*. It is normally served with meals in small bowls and eaten with the fried puffy breads called pooris, but I strain out all the leaves and seeds that would normally float in it and serve it as a soup. My friends and family love it. It needs to be served hot, as it is thickened with very nutritious chickpea flour that does not behave well when it is cold. It is very quick and easy to make, since it uses canned mango puree. One of India's finest mangoes is the Alphonso, and it is canned Alphonso puree that you should look for. All Indian grocers carry it. The brand I like and use is Ratna. It comes slightly sweetened.

Conveniently, the 30-ounce Ratna cans hold exactly 3 cups, just what you need here.

½ cup plain yogurt, preferably made with acidophilus

2 tablespoons chickpea flour

One 30-ounce can pureed Alphonso mango (3 cups)

1¼–1½ teaspoons salt

½ teaspoon sugar, or to taste

⅛ teaspoon ground turmeric

¾ teaspoon ground cumin

¾ teaspoon ground coriander

¼ teaspoon red chili powder

2 tablespoons peanut or olive oil

½ teaspoon whole black or brown mustard seeds

½ teaspoon whole cumin seeds

⅛ teaspoon whole fenugreek seeds

10–15 fresh curry leaves, if available

1–2 bird's-eye chilies with long slits cut along their lengths but not to the edges

1. Put the yogurt in a small bowl. Slowly add 1 cup water, whisking as you go.

2. Put the chickpea flour in a slightly larger bowl. Pour in just a little of the yogurt-water mixture and whisk to a very smooth paste. Slowly add the rest of the mixture, whisking as you go. (If there are any lumps, strain the mixture.) Set aside.

3. Put the mango puree in an even bigger bowl. Add the salt, sugar, turmeric, cumin, coriander, chili powder, and 1½ cups water. Mix well. Set aside.

4. Select the SAUTÉ setting on your Instant Pot, set to More, and pour in the oil. When the screen says Hot, put in the mustard and cumin seeds. As soon as the mustard seeds pop, a matter of seconds, add the fenugreek seeds and curry leaves. A second later, pour in the mango mixture and add the green chili or chilies. Stir well.

5. Hit CANCEL to reset the cooking program, then cook on HIGH PRESSURE with the lid sealed, setting the timer for 3 minutes. When the time is up, let the pressure release naturally for 5 minutes and then release the rest of it manually.

6. Open the lid carefully, venting the steam away from you. Stir the yogurt-chickpea flour mixture and pour it in. Stir well. Hit CANCEL and then select the SAUTÉ setting and set to More. Once the soup is boiling, set the SAUTÉ setting to Less and continue to cook for about 3 minutes. Strain the soup just before serving, allowing the spices to release their flavors for as long as possible.

LAMB OR CHICKEN MULLIGATAWNY SOUP

SERVES 4–6

Based on the *milagu-tannir,* or pepper-water, of the South Indian Tamils, this much-loved soup was created by the Anglo-Indian community in India. It is their Sunday treat, eaten for lunch with rice on the side. The rice—exactly as much as one wants—gets dunked in. Of course, there are squeezes of lime juice as well. It is a soup that the whole country has come to love. I happen to be quite addicted to it myself.

If you wish to use chicken instead of lamb, buy ¾ pound boned and skinned thighs, cut them up, brown them like the lamb pieces, and then cook them at **low pressure** for 2 minutes, releasing the pressure manually. Use only chicken stock for the liquid.

Serve with Plain Basmati Rice (page 116).

5 tablespoons chickpea flour

6 cups chicken stock

1 teaspoon ground cumin

1 teaspoon ground coriander

¼ teaspoon ground turmeric

¼ teaspoon chili powder

1 teaspoon hot curry powder
   (I like Bolst's)

2 tablespoons peanut or olive
   oil

¾ pound boneless lamb from
   the shoulder, cut into ¾-
   inch pieces

1 tablespoon peeled fresh
   ginger grated to a pulp

4 cloves garlic, peeled and
   crushed to a pulp

Salt

1 tablespoon lime or lemon
   juice, plus wedges to serve

1. Put the chickpea flour in a bowl. Take 1 cup of the stock, then very slowly add some of it to make a thick paste, breaking all lumps against the sides of the bowl. Add the remainder of the 1 cup once lumps are gone. (Save the other 5 cups of stock for later.)

2. Put the cumin, coriander, turmeric, chili powder, and curry powder in a small bowl and set aside.

3. Select the SAUTÉ setting on your Instant Pot and set to More. When the screen says HOT, swirl in the oil. A few seconds later, add 8 or 9 of the lamb pieces and brown them a little on all sides. Remove them with a slotted spoon to a plate. Brown all the lamb this way, in batches.

4. Now put the ginger and garlic into the Instant Pot. Stir once or twice. Add all the spices from

the small bowl. Stir a few times, and then stir in the remaining 5 cups of stock. Add all the browned meat and its juices back in, along with ¼ teaspoon salt if the stock was salted; if it was not, start with ¾ teaspoon salt and add more later if you need it. Stir. Hit CANCEL to reset the cooking program. Cook at HIGH PRESSURE for 15 minutes and then let the pressure fall naturally. Hit CANCEL. Remove the lid, carefully making sure that the steam is venting away from you. Select the SAUTÉ setting and set to Normal. Stir, and check the salt. Stir the chickpea flour mixture and pour it in, stirring as the soup thickens. Let it cook gently for 2–3 minutes. Add the lime or lemon juice and stir. Serve with lime or lemon wedges.

MUNG DAL, RICE, AND CABBAGE SOUP

SERVES 6-8

This may well be my all-time-favorite soup. It is based on one of the oldest Indian dishes, *khicherie* (from whence the British got "kedgerie"), which has been cooked in India for several thousand years. Khicherie, at its simplest, is rice and mung dal (hulled and split mung beans) cooked together and served with a dollop of butter or ghee.

This soup is something I made up. In my refrigerator, I had a little leftover khicherie and a little leftover Indian cabbage that I had sautéed with fennel seeds, cumin seeds, shallots, and chili powder. For lunch one day, I just put the two together, adding enough water to transform them into a soup. Now I make this soup all the time! The Instant Pot makes it all very easy.

Dals tend to thicken as they sit, so when reheating, you will probably need to thin this out. You can use water or any stock you like.

1 cup mung dal (hulled and split mung beans)

½ cup basmati rice

3 tablespoons peanut or olive oil

¼ teaspoon ground asafetida

½ teaspoon whole cumin seeds

¼ teaspoon whole fennel seeds

2 cups cabbage (¼ medium cabbage) cut lengthways into long, thin shreds

½ cup shallots cut into long, thin slices (like the cabbage)

2 teaspoons finely grated peeled fresh ginger

½ teaspoon ground coriander

½ teaspoon ground cumin

½–¾ teaspoon chili powder

Salt

1 teaspoon ground turmeric

½ packed cup chopped green coriander leaves

1 medium tomato, peeled and cut into ½-inch dice

1 tablespoon lemon juice

1. Put the mung dal and rice in a bowl. Wash in several changes of water and drain. Set aside.

2. Select the SAUTÉ setting on your Instant Pot and set to More. Pour in the oil. When the screen says Hot, add the asafetida and the cumin seeds. A second later, put in the fennel seeds. Wait another second and add the cabbage and

shallots. Stir and sauté for 6–7 minutes, until you see a little browning. Turn down heat to Normal. Add the ginger, coriander, cumin, chili powder, and ¼ teaspoon salt. Stir and sauté for another 2–3 minutes. Hit CANCEL to reset the cooking program. Spoon out all the cabbage and put it in a bowl.

3. Empty the drained mung dal and rice into the inner container of the Instant Pot, making sure that no grains are left on the lip. Add 10 cups water, the turmeric, and 1½ teaspoons salt. Close and seal the lid, and set the PRESSURE RELEASE to SEALING. Cook at HIGH PRESSURE, setting the timer for 15 minutes. Let the pressure release naturally.

4. Remove the lid carefully. Select the SAUTÉ setting and set to Normal. When the screen says Hot, add the cabbage and the chopped green coriander leaves. Cook for 10 minutes, add the tomatoes and lemon juice, and mix and taste for balance of flavors. Cook another 2–3 minutes.

BEANS

BUTTERY DAL

Dal Makkhani

SERVES 6

The Indian state of Punjab is known for the dairy that is consumed in generous amounts by its farming population. (Perhaps you will not be surprised to learn that today it is immigrant Punjabi farmers who care for the cows that produce the milk for Parmigiano-Reggiano cheese around the city of Parma in Italy.) More than half of Punjabi farmers are vegetarian and seem to thrive on local yogurt, cheese (paneer), lassis, and butter.

This dal is made with a mixture of red kidney beans—an early import from the Americas—and an ancient Indian bean known as whole urad or ma. The dish is called Dal Makkhani, or Buttery Dal, because of all the white butter that is used to enrich it. You can use as much "enrichment" as you choose.

It is traditionally served with Indian flatbreads—naans, chapatis, tandoori rotis, and parathas. Whole-wheat pita bread works well too. Onion-Tomato Salad (page 138) and a vegetable dish served on the side would complete the meal.

1 cup whole urad with skin
    (also called *sabut ma*)
½ cup dried red kidney beans
    (called *rajma* in Indian
    stores)
Salt
4 teaspoons peeled fresh
    ginger grated to a pulp
1 tablespoon crushed garlic
1 cup pureed or strained
    tomatoes or passata
¼–½ teaspoon chili powder
1 tablespoon butter, plus more
    if needed
½ cup heavy cream
1 teaspoon My Garam Masala
    (page 154)

FOR THE TARKA

2 tablespoons peanut oil or ghee
About 6 very thin rounds of
    onions, halved
¼ teaspoon bright red paprika
    mixed with ¼ teaspoon
    chili powder

1. Wash the beans and soak them overnight in water that covers them generously. Drain them the following day.

2. Put the beans in the Instant Pot. Add 1 teaspoon salt, the ginger, garlic, tomatoes, chili powder, and 4 cups water. Close and seal the lid, then cook on **HIGH PRESSURE** for 30 minutes,

before letting the pressure drop by itself. Hit CANCEL to reset the cooking program. Open the lid carefully, venting the steam away from you. Stir the dal. Using a potato masher, crush the dal as much as you can. Taste, adding another ½ teaspoon salt as needed.

3. Select the SAUTÉ setting and set to Normal. Stir in the 1 tablespoon butter, cream, and garam masala. When the dal is heated through, you may put it in a serving dish and add another dollop of butter on top, or you may use the tarka (see below).

Tarka: Put the oil or ghee in a small frying pan over medium heat. When hot, arrange the onions in a single layer. Stir and fry them, turning now and then, until they turn reddish gold and crisp. Sprinkle the paprika mixture over the top and quickly pour all the contents of the pan over the beans, spreading it out over the surface. Cover with a towel or extra lid to trap the aromas.

SIMPLE MUNG DAL

Tarkay Ki Moong Dal
SERVES 4

This is soul food to most North Indians. Made with just native Indian mung beans, hulled and split, or with a half-and-half mixture of these and masoor dal (hulled and split red lentils), this dal is cooked into a thick, soupy texture and then eaten with rice or local flatbreads along with vegetables, yogurt relishes, and chutneys. Mung dal is supposed to be the easiest dal to digest, hence it is the first one given to babies and is often the last dal eaten through very old age. This is what my little granddaughter ate while my daughter, Sakina, and I were filming in South India for three months. For her, it was cooked very simply, with just a little turmeric and very little salt. She was six months old at the time and just lapped it up. For most of us, however, the dal is enriched with a "tarka," the final seasoning that can include chilies and onions and cumin seeds and the digestive asafetida.

FOR THE MUNG DAL

1 cup mung dal (hulled and
   split mung beans), washed
   in several changes of water
   and then drained
½ teaspoon ground turmeric
¾–1 teaspoon salt

FOR THE TARKA

2 tablespoons peanut or
   olive oil or ghee (clarified
   butter)
⅛ teaspoon ground asafetida
½ teaspoon whole cumin
   seeds
1–2 dried hot red chilies

1. Combine the mung dal, turmeric, salt, and 3½ cups water in the inner container of the Instant Pot. Close and seal the lid and cook at **LOW PRESSURE** for 10 minutes. Let the pressure release naturally for 3 minutes and then release the remaining pressure manually. Remove the lid carefully, venting the steam away from you. Stir and mash the dal either against the sides of the pot or by using a potato masher. Add more hot water if a thinner consistency is desired.

2. Put the oil or ghee in a small frying pan set over medium-high heat. When hot, put in, in very quick succession, first the asafetida, then the cumin seeds, and finally the red chilies. As soon as the chilies darken, pour the oil or ghee and the spices over the cooked dal. Cover with a towel or other free lid to trap aromas.

MUNG DAL WITH SPINACH

Saag Wali Moong

SERVES 4

Dals can be combined with almost anything — meat, fish, and most vegetables. Here mung dal (hulled and split mung beans) is cooked with spinach, in a very popular combination. Serve with rice or flatbreads.

FOR THE MUNG DAL

1 cup mung dal (hulled and
   split mung beans), washed
   in several changes of water
   and then drained

½ teaspoon ground turmeric

1 teaspoon salt

1 medium stick cinnamon

1 teaspoon peeled fresh ginger
   grated to a pulp

6 ounces fresh spinach (I
   use baby spinach), finely
   chopped

¼ teaspoon My Garam Masala
   (page 154)

FOR THE TARKA

2 tablespoons peanut or olive
   oil or ghee

1–2 dried hot red chilies

2 garlic cloves, peeled and
   halved lengthways

FOR SERVING, OPTIONAL

A little grated nutmeg

Lime or lemon wedges

1. Combine the mung dal, turmeric, salt, cinnamon stick, ginger, spinach, and 3½ cups water in the inner container of the Instant Pot. Close and seal the lid. Cook at **LOW PRESSURE** for 10 minutes and then release the steam manually. Hit **CANCEL** to reset the cooking program and remove the lid carefully, venting the steam away from you. Add the garam masala and stir it in. Mash the dal with a potato masher.

2. Put the oil or ghee into a small frying pan set over medium-high heat. When hot, add the chili or chilies. Turn the chili or chilies quickly as one side darkens. Add the garlic, turning the pieces over until they brown lightly. Quickly pour the oil and seasonings over the dal. Cover with a towel or extra lid to trap aromas.

3. Grate a little nutmeg over the top when serving. Lime or lemon wedges may be offered as well. You may need to add water when reheating and serving if the dal gets too thick.

PLAIN CHICKPEAS

Saaday Chanay
MAKES 2 CUPS

Sometimes you just need plain cooked chickpeas: to strew into a salad, to put in a soup, or to add to a stew. Each chickpea has a skin around it that gets slightly loosened after cooking. It then comes off and becomes part of the sauce. You can leave it, and enjoy the roughage it provides, or you can remove it – somewhat laborious work – and enjoy a cleaner salad, soup, or or stew. In this book I use the skinned chickpeas in a soup (Cold Yogurt Soup with Chickpeas, Cucumbers, and Tomatoes, page 2). Here is how you prepare the chickpeas:

1 cup dried chickpeas

¾ teaspoon salt

1. Soak the chickpeas overnight in water that covers them generously. Drain them the next morning and put them into the inner container of the Instant Pot along with the salt and 2 cups of water. Close and seal the lid and cook at HIGH PRESSURE, setting the timer for 3 minutes. Then let the pressure drop naturally for 3 minutes before releasing it manually.

2. Remove the lid, venting the steam away from you. Wearing oven mitts, lift out the inner pot and let it cool off a bit. Now strain the chickpeas, saving the cooking liquid for stock or other uses. Remove any loose skins. These are your plain cooked chickpeas. To remove all the skins, more work is required.

4. Put the chickpeas in a large bowl. Fill the bowl with water. Picking up one chickpea at a time, slip off its skin and set it aside. (It's best

to do this sitting down, perhaps while watching television, or get others to join in.) Do all the chickpeas this way. Store the chickpeas and their liquid separately in covered containers.

USING UNSOAKED CHICKPEAS

I find that soaking produces evenly soft-cooked chickpeas. But what if you have forgotten to soak them overnight? Here is how you do it:

1 cup dried chickpeas
¾ teaspoon salt

1. Put the dried chickpeas into the inner container of the Instant Pot along with the salt and 2½ cups of water. Close and seal the lid. Cook at **HIGH PRESSURE**, setting the timer for 50 minutes, and then let the pressure release naturally by itself. If the chickpeas are still not done, repeat the process for another 5 minutes under **HIGH PRESSURE**.

2. Remove the lid, venting the steam away from you. Wearing oven mitts, lift out the inner pot and let it cool off a bit. Now strain the chickpeas, saving the cooking liquid for stock or other uses. Remove any loose skins. For removing all the skins, follow the recipe above.

EVERYDAY CHICKPEAS

Ghar Kay Chanay

SERVES 4

This is what most North Indians cook as their everyday chickpea dish. I have not removed any of the chickpea skins here.

You may serve it with Indian or any other flatbreads and a yogurt relish, or serve it in individual bowls topped with the Cucumber, Onion, and Tomato Salad (page 137).

There is another way to serve it in a bowl – and this what the street snack-sellers in North India sometimes do: they top the chickpeas first with a little plain yogurt that is lightly whipped into a smooth sauce. On this yogurt they sprinkle some salt, ground roasted cumin seeds (for my technique, see page 152), and a little chili powder. On top of that they drizzle just a little Easy Tamarind Chutney (page 142) and scatter chopped green coriander leaves over the very top. Then they hand it to you to gobble up!

As for the chaat masala I have used here, it is sold at all Indian grocers and contains, among other things, dried sour mango powder and black salt.

1½ cups dried chickpeas

3 tablespoons vegetable oil

1 large onion, finely chopped

One 3-inch piece peeled fresh ginger, either very finely chopped or finely grated

4 cloves garlic, peeled and either very finely chopped or crushed to a pulp

1 finely chopped bird's-eye chili or about ½ of a jalapeño, finely chopped with seeds

¼ teaspoon chili powder, or more as desired

1 teaspoon ground cumin

1 teaspoon ground coriander

¼ teaspoon ground turmeric

1 cup peeled and chopped tomatoes (canned is fine)

1 teaspoon salt

1 teaspoon My Garam Masala (page 154)

1 teaspoon chaat masala

1 tablespoon lemon juice, or more as desired

Cilantro leaves, for garnishing

1. Soak the chickpeas in water that covers them by about 4 inches and leave overnight. Drain before cooking.

2. Select the SAUTÉ setting on your Instant Pot and set to More, setting the timer for 30

minutes. When the screen says Hot, swirl in the oil. Then put in all the onions. Stir and cook them for 5–7 minutes or until lightly browned. Add the ginger and garlic. Stir and cook for another 2 minutes. Add the green chilies, the chili powder, cumin, coriander, and turmeric and stir a few times. Now put in the tomatoes. Stir and cook for 3–4 minutes or until the tomatoes are reduced and thick. Add the drained chickpeas, salt, and 2 cups water. Press CANCEL to reset the cooking program.

3. Close and seal the lid. Cook at HIGH PRESSURE, setting the timer for 3 minutes, and then let the pressure drop naturally for 3 minutes. Release the remaining pressure manually. Remove the lid carefully, venting the steam away from you. Add the garam masala, the chaat masala, and the lemon juice. Stir gently to mix. Serve hot or at room temperature, garnished with just the cilantro or as suggested in the headnote.

CHICKPEAS IN A GINGERY TOMATO SAUCE

Adrak Aur Timatar Wala Chana

SERVES 4

Sometimes, after I boil chickpeas, I like to remove the skins only partially so I have a relatively clean sauce but retain some of the roughage. That is what I have done here.

These chickpeas can be served as part of an Indian meal that includes meat, vegetables, and rice or flatbreads, or they may be served in a bowl topped with a little yogurt, and with crusty bread and a salad offered on the side.

1½ cups dried chickpeas

Salt

3 tablespoons peanut or olive oil

¼ teaspoon whole cumin seeds

¼ teaspoon nigella seeds (known as kalonji in Indian markets)

1 tablespoon peeled fresh ginger grated to a pulp

4 cloves garlic, peeled and crushed to a pulp

1 cup pureed tomatoes (or passata or strained tomatoes)

⅛–½ teaspoon chili powder

1 tablespoon lemon juice

2 tablespoons chopped cilantro leaves

Green chilies of any heat you desire, chopped

1. Soak the chickpeas overnight in water that covers them generously. Drain them the next morning. Put them into the inner container of the Instant Pot along with 2 cups water and 1 teaspoon salt. Cook at HIGH PRESSURE, setting the timer for 3 minutes, and then let the pressure release by itself for 3 minutes. Release the remaining pressure manually. Remove the lid carefully, venting the steam away from you. Wearing oven mitts, remove the inner pot and let it cool off a bit. Strain the chickpeas, saving the liquid. Put the chickpeas in a large bowl. Fill the bowl with water and rub the chickpeas gently to remove the skins. Pour off the water and skins, then add more water and repeat the process a few times. You won't get every skin, but you will get the looser ones. That is the aim here. Drain and save the chickpeas in a bowl or colander. Meanwhile, wash and dry the inner pot and put it back in its housing.

2. Select the SAUTÉ setting and set to More. When the screen says Hot, swirl in the oil. Wait

a few seconds and add the cumin and nigella seeds. Stir a few times. Add the ginger and garlic. Stir for a minute or until they turn golden. Add the tomato puree and stir for a minute. Add 1 cup of the saved chickpea liquid, the chickpeas, ½ teaspoon salt, and the chili powder. Turn the SAUTÉ mode to Normal and stir gently for 2 minutes. Hit CANCEL. Add the lemon juice and stir it in. Serve topped with the cilantro and, if you desire, the green chilies.

BLACK-EYED PEAS WITH MUSHROOMS

Lobhia Aur Khumbi

SERVES 6

There is so much that can be done with black-eyed peas. You can cook them when they are green; you can make fritters with them when they are dried. You can also use them as a daily dal, and this is one such recipe. Here they are cooked with mushrooms. Serve this dish in small individual bowls if it is to be eaten with flatbreads, or serve over rice. Sometimes for lunch, I just put some of it in a small bowl, make a quick Avocado-Radish Salad (page 135), and eat it with some whole-grain bread.

1¾ cups dried black-eyed peas

3 tablespoons peanut or olive oil

½ teaspoon whole cumin seeds

1 medium cinnamon stick

1 medium onion, chopped

3 cloves garlic, peeled and finely chopped

½ pound white mushrooms, cut crossways into ⅛-inch-thick slices

4 medium tomatoes, peeled and chopped (canned are fine), about 1 cup

1 teaspoon ground cumin

2 teaspoons ground coriander

½ teaspoon ground turmeric

¼–½ teaspoon chili powder

1¼ teaspoons salt

Cilantro leaves, for garnishing

1. Soak the black-eyed peas overnight in water that covers them generously and drain before cooking. Select the SAUTÉ setting and set to More. When the screen says Hot, swirl in the oil. Wait a few seconds and put in the cumin seeds and cinnamon stick. Stir a few times. Add the onions and stir and cook for 2 minutes. Then add the garlic and continue to stir and cook until the onions start to brown a little. Add the mushrooms. Stir and sauté another 2 minutes, until the mushrooms look glossy. Now put in the tomatoes, ground cumin, coriander, turmeric, and chili powder. Stir and cook for 2–3 minutes. Add the drained black-eyed peas, salt, and 3½ cups water. Hit CANCEL to reset the cooking program.

2. Close and seal the lid. Cook at LOW PRESSURE for 7 minutes and then let the pressure release naturally for 10 minutes. Release the remaining pressure manually. Hit CANCEL. Take off the lid carefully, venting the steam away from you. You may thicken the sauce by cooking it some more using the SAUTÉ function set to More, but I like to leave it the way it is. All beans tend to thicken as they sit.

RED LENTILS COOKED IN A MUSLIM STYLE

Musalmani Masoor

SERVES 4

Both Hindus and Muslims in India cook red lentils. But they cook them differently. Hindus like to put in asafetida, a digestive, and Muslims, who never eat asafetida, prefer to use garlic for a similar strong earthy aroma. As most dals tend to thicken as they sit, you might need to add more water when you reheat it.

This dal would be considered an everyday dish. It is served with either rice or an Indian flatbread. In India, if eaten with flatbreads, lentils tend to be cooked so they stay a bit thick and are usually served in individual bowls. Also on the table would be a vegetable, such as a green bean or cauliflower dish, and a yogurt relish. A meat dish, perhaps the Rajasthani Red Braised Lamb (page 104), might also be served in households that eat meat.

FOR THE LENTILS

1 cup split red lentils (masoor dal), washed in several changes of water and then drained

½ teaspoon ground turmeric

2 cloves garlic, peeled

1 green bird's-eye chili with a slit cut along part of its length

¾ teaspoon salt, or to taste

FOR THE TARKA

2 tablespoons peanut or olive oil

1 dried hot red chili

⅛ cup finely sliced shallots or onions

1 clove garlic, peeled and cut into thin slices

FOR SERVING

Lime or lemon wedges

1. Combine the drained red lentils, turmeric, garlic, green chili, salt, and 3½ cups water in the inner container of the Instant Pot. Close and seal the lid. Cook at LOW PRESSURE for 8 minutes. Release the pressure manually. Remove the lid carefully, venting the steam away from you. Stir and mash the lentils either against the sides of the pot or by using a potato masher, making sure that you have mashed the garlic cloves into the dal. What remains of the green chili should be removed. Add more hot water, if needed, to get the consistency you desire.

2. Put the oil into a small frying pan set over medium-high heat. When hot, put in the red chili. It will turn dark quickly. Turn it and quickly add the shallots and garlic. Stir and fry them until they brown lightly. Pour the oil and seasonings over the red lentils. Cover with a towel or extra lid to trap aromas. Stir the seasonings in just before serving. Offer lime or lemon slices for squeezing on the dal.

BROWN LENTILS WITH ZUCCHINI

Sabut Masoor Aur Zucchini

SERVES 4–6

Zucchini are not commonly grown in India, but there are dozens of similar summer squashes there that are cooked with dals.

All dals thicken as they sit. Do thin this out with water, as needed. It should have an easy-flowing consistency and never be like lava. You can mix in a dollop of butter when you serve.

3 tablespoons peanut or olive oil

1 medium zucchini, cut in half lengthways and then crossways into 1-inch sections

Salt

Freshly ground pepper

Chili powder

½ teaspoon whole cumin seeds

¼ teaspoon whole mustard seeds

1 dried hot red chili

1 cup chopped onions

1 large clove garlic, peeled and finely chopped

2 teaspoons ground coriander

1 teaspoon ground cumin

¼ teaspoon ground turmeric

1 cup peeled and chopped tomatoes

1–2 fresh hot green chilies, chopped

1 cup brown lentils or whole masoor dal

½ cup chopped cilantro

1. Select the **SAUTÉ** setting on your Instant Pot and set to More, setting the timer for 30 minutes. When the screen says Hot, swirl in the oil. Put in the zucchini pieces. Stir them around until lightly browned on all sides.

2. Remove zucchini and put them on a plate. Sprinkle lightly with salt, pepper, and chili powder. Mix and set aside.

3. Put the cumin seeds, mustard seeds, and red chili into the Instant Pot. Stir a few times until the chili is dark on both sides. Put in the onions. Stir and cook until lightly browned, about 5 minutes. Add the garlic and stir for a minute, then add the ground coriander, ground cumin, ground turmeric, and ¼ teaspoon chili powder. Stir once, add the tomatoes and green chilies, and stir for a minute. Add the lentils, cilantro, 1 teaspoon salt, and 4 cups water. Press **CANCEL** to reset the cooking program.

4. Close and seal the lid. Cook on **HIGH PRESSURE** for 15 minutes. Let the pressure drop by itself. Remove the lid carefully, venting the steam away from you. Taste for salt. Add the zucchini to the pot and stir it in. Select the **SAUTÉ** setting, set to Normal, and simmer for a minute.

GUJARATI HOT, SWEET, AND SOUR RED KIDNEY BEANS

Gujarati Rajma

SERVES 6

I got this delightful recipe from a Gujarati family living in South Africa. You may serve it with any flatbread or with rice. A green bean, kale, or spinach dish would be a perfect addition to the meal.

1½ cups dried red kidney beans

3 tablespoons peanut or olive oil

⅛ teaspoon ground asafetida

½ teaspoon black or brown mustard seeds

½ teaspoon whole cumin seeds

2 dried hot red chilies

10–15 fresh curry leaves, if available

1 cup peeled and finely chopped tomatoes, fresh or canned

¼ teaspoon ground turmeric

1 teaspoon ground coriander

1 teaspoon ground cumin

1–2 fresh hot green chilies (like bird's-eye), finely chopped

1 clove garlic, peeled and crushed to a pulp

1 teaspoon peeled fresh ginger grated to a pulp

1 teaspoon sugar

1 teaspoon salt

1. Wash the beans and soak them overnight in water that covers them generously. Drain them the next day just before cooking.

2. Select the SAUTÉ setting on your Instant Pot and set to More for 30 minutes. When the screen says Hot, add oil, put in the asafetida, the mustard seeds, the cumin seeds, and the red chilies. Stir until the mustard seeds pop and the chilies darken. Add the curry leaves. They will splatter, so stand back. Stir once and add the tomatoes, turmeric, coriander, cumin, green chilies, garlic, and ginger. Stir and cook for 2–3 minutes. Add the sugar and salt. Stir and cook another minute. Add the drained beans and 3½ cups water. Hit CANCEL to reset the cooking program. Close and seal the lid. Cook at HIGH PRESSURE for 30 minutes and then let the pressure drop naturally. Hit CANCEL again. Open the lid carefully, venting the steam away from you.

3. Select the SAUTÉ setting and set to More. You may thicken the sauce by cooking for 3–5 minutes more, stirring as you do so. Remember, the sauce will also thicken a bit as it sits.

VEGETABLES

BEETS IN A DELHI-STYLE TOMATO SAUCE

SERVES 6

The beets here are served with a rather delicious thin, hot, and sour sauce. Thus we tend to serve this dish in small, individual bowls, and eat it with a spoon. I can never forget how my father, who loved both his meat and this dish, took so much joy in combining the sauces of both the day's meat dish and the beets and eating them together. I often do the same myself. You can also do the same with some dal and the beets. You need some Indian flatbread or even a baguette to sop up all the good juices! For a vegetarian meal, you could serve these beets, a dal, some rice, and the Cucumber, Onion, and Tomato Salad (page 137).

This recipe requires strained or pureed tomatoes, which you can buy in bottles at many supermarkets. You may also use a can of pureed tomatoes.

2 tablespoons peanut or olive oil

⅛ teaspoon ground asafetida

½ teaspoon whole cumin seeds

1–2 hot red chilies (1 for medium heat, 2 for more)

1½ pounds beets without leaves (I used 2 largish beets), peeled and cut into ½-inch dice

1 cup tomato passata

½ teaspoon ground turmeric

1 teaspoon salt

1. Put the oil in the inner container of the Instant Pot and select the **SAUTÉ** setting set to More. When the screen says Hot, put in the asafetida. Let it sizzle for a second, then add the cumin seeds and the red chili or chilies. When the chili darkens on one side, quickly turn it over and immediately add the beets, stirring and sautéing them for 2 minutes. Add the passata, 1¾ cups water, turmeric, and salt. Stir to mix.

2. Hit **CANCEL** to reset the cooking program and close and seal the lid. Cook at **HIGH PRESSURE** for 20 minutes and then let the pressure drop naturally.

GREEN BEANS STIR-FRIED IN A SOUTH INDIAN STYLE

SERVES 4

South Indian kitchens contain all manner of steamers and pressure cookers that are used to cook everything from rice to beans to noodles and vegetables. Very often vegetables are just steamed and then quickly sautéed with mustard seeds, chilies, and curry leaves. One seasoning that is often added to this list is not really a seasoning at all but is made to behave like one. It is a dal—a split pea known as urad dal. If you do not have it, you may use yellow split peas or mung dal instead. When allowed to brown, it provides a nutty flavor. These beans may be served at almost any meal.

1 pound green beans, cut into 1-inch pieces

3 tablespoons peanut or olive oil

⅛ teaspoon ground asafetida

½ teaspoon whole black or brown mustard seeds

½ teaspoon urad dal (see headnote)

2 dried hot red chilies

10 fresh curry leaves, if available

¾ teaspoon salt

⅛–¼ teaspoon chili powder

1½ teaspoons lemon juice

1. Add 1 cup water to the Instant pot. Put the cut green beans into a steamer basket and set it over the water, then close and seal the lid. Select the STEAM setting set to low pressure and cook for 1 minute. When the display says 1, start venting the steam manually. When all the steam has been vented, open the lid carefully, venting all the remaining steam away from you. Hit CANCEL to reset the cooking program. Wearing oven mitts, lift the basket carefully and leave the beans to cool. Meanwhile, wash the inner pot and dry it. Put it back in the Instant Pot.

2. When the beans have cooled off, select the SAUTÉ setting and set to More. When the screen says Hot, swirl in the oil. A few seconds later, put in the asafetida, mustard seeds, urad dal, and red chilies. Stir until the dal turns reddish and the chilies darken. Add the curry leaves. They will splatter, so stand back. Now add the green beans, salt, and chili powder. Stir and cook for another 2 minutes. Add the lemon juice and mix it in. Taste for balance of flavors. Hit CANCEL.

CARROTS AND PEAS WITH SESAME SEEDS

SERVES 4

A nourishing, delicious, everyday dish that can be served with most meals. I have used frozen peas here. If fresh ones are in season and you wish to use them, steam them along with the carrots first.

1 pound carrots, peeled and cut into ⅓-inch-thick rounds

2 tablespoons peanut or olive oil

⅛ teaspoon ground asafetida

½ teaspoon whole cumin seeds

1 teaspoon sesame seeds

1 cup frozen peas, defrosted (or fresh, see headnote)

1 teaspoon peeled and very finely grated fresh ginger

½ teaspoon ground cumin

½ teaspoon ground coriander

⅛–½ teaspoon chili powder

¼–½ teaspoon salt, according to taste

1. Pour 1 cup water into the inner container of the Instant Pot and then set the steaming basket on top of it. Put the cut carrots (and fresh peas, if using) into the basket and close and seal the lid. Select the STEAM setting, set to low pressure, and cook for 2 minutes. When the display says 2, start releasing the steam manually. When all the steam has been vented, open the lid carefully, venting the remaining steam away from you. Hit CANCEL to reset the cooking program. Wearing oven mitts, lift the basket out carefully and leave the carrots to cool. Meanwhile, wash the inner pot and dry it. Put it back into the Instant Pot.

2. When the carrots have cooled off, select the SAUTÉ setting and set to More. When the screen says Hot, swirl in the oil. A few seconds later, put in the asafetida, cumin seeds, and sesame seeds. When the sesame seeds turn golden, add the carrots, peas, ginger, ground cumin, ground coriander, chili powder, and salt. Stir and cook for 2–3 minutes. Taste for balance of flavors, adding more salt and chili powder if needed. Hit CANCEL.

SWEET, HOT, AND SOUR EGGPLANTS

SERVES 4–6

My family loves this eggplant dish. As most of my children do not like raisins in cooked savory foods, I tend to leave them out when cooking for them, but I certainly like to include them when cooking for my husband, myself, and invited guests. You could serve this dish as a vegetable course with a main meal or with crusty bread as a first course. It is also good cold, served almost as a salad. This dish cooks easily and quickly in the Instant Pot.

4 tablespoons olive or peanut oil

⅛ teaspoon ground asafetida

½ teaspoon whole brown or black mustard seeds

½ teaspoon whole cumin seeds

1 teaspoon whole nigella seeds

3 tablespoons golden raisins

2 cups chopped onions

3 cloves garlic, peeled and very finely chopped

1¼ pounds slim Japanese eggplants, cut crossways into 1-inch segments, or baby Italian eggplants, cut in half lengthways and then crossways into 1-inch segments

⅔ cup tomato puree, passata, or strained tomatoes

1 cup chicken stock or water

1 teaspoon salt

Lots of freshly ground pepper

¼–½ teaspoon chili powder

Possible garnishing options, if desired: Fresh cilantro leaves, chopped up just before serving, or fresh mint leaves cut into fine slivers just before serving

1. Select the **SAUTÉ** setting and set to More. Pour in the oil. When the screen says Hot, put in first the asafetida, then, a second later, the mustard seeds, cumin seeds, and nigella. Stir once and add the raisins. Stir. When they swell up, a matter of seconds, immediately put in the onions. Stir and sauté for about 2 minutes or until onions have softened a bit. Add the garlic and stir another minute, then put in all the eggplant chunks. Stir and sauté for 4 minutes or until onions have browned a bit and the eggplant skin has lost its color. Add the tomato puree, stock or water, salt, pepper, and chili powder. Stir. Hit **CANCEL** to reset the cooking program.

2. Close and seal the lid. Cook on **HIGH PRESSURE** for 3 minutes, then release the pressure manually. Take off the lid carefully, venting the remaining steam away from you.

CAULIFLOWER WITH CILANTRO AND GINGER

SERVES 4–5

This may be served with a lamb or poultry dish along with rice or a flatbread. It is light and lemony and is one of my favorite dishes for entertaining. In the summer, you may serve it cold as part of a buffet.

¾ teaspoon salt

2 teaspoons ground coriander

1 teaspoon ground cumin

½ teaspoon ground turmeric

½ teaspoon My Garam Masala (page 154)

Freshly ground black pepper, a generous grinding

⅛–¼ teaspoon chili powder

3 tablespoons peanut or olive oil

¼ teaspoon whole black or brown mustard seeds

¼ teaspoon whole cumin seeds

One 1¾-pound head cauliflower, with thick central stem and leaves discarded and the head broken into florets (each floret should have a stem and be about 1½–2 inches long and about 1½ inches in diameter at its head)

1½ teaspoons peeled and finely grated fresh ginger

1 lightly packed cup chopped cilantro leaves

½–1 fresh hot green bird's-eye chili, finely chopped

1 tablespoon lemon juice

1. Combine the salt, ground coriander, ground cumin, turmeric, garam masala, black pepper, and chili powder in a small bowl and set aside.

2. Select the SAUTÉ setting on your Instant Pot and set to More for 30 minutes. When the screen says Hot, pour in the oil. A few seconds later, scatter in the mustard seeds and cumin seeds. When the mustard seeds start popping, a matter of seconds, put in all the cauliflower. Stir the cauliflower now and then for 5 minutes. Add the ginger and give a few quick stirs, then add the dry spice mixture and stir a few more times. Add the cilantro and green chilies, give a few more stirs, then put in the lemon juice and stir once. Add ¾ cup water and hit CANCEL to stop the cooking process.

3. Close and seal the lid. Set the pot to LOW PRESSURE for 1 minute. As soon as the screen

says 1, hit CANCEL and quickly release all the steam manually. Open the lid, venting the remaining steam away from you. Select the SAUTÉ setting set to More and boil off most of the liquid, stirring gently from the bottom as you do so. Taste for balance of flavors. Wearing oven mitts, lift out the inner pot from the outer pot to stop the cauliflower from cooking any more.

KALE COOKED IN A KASHMIRI STYLE

SERVES 4

Kashmiris cook a lot of hardy greens very similar to collard greens and kale. They like to cook them in mustard oil, but you may use any oil of your choice. This dish is eaten with rice in Kashmir. That seems perfect to me, as the rice absorbs kale juices very efficiently.

1 pound kale (weight with
    stems and veins)

3 tablespoons mustard oil

1–2 dried hot red chilies

2 good-sized cloves garlic,
    peeled and cut lengthways
    into 3–4 pieces each

¾ teaspoon salt, or to taste

1. Stand up the kale leaves, one at a time. Cut off and save just the leafy section. You can discard the tougher stems and central veins. Coarsely chop up the greens.

2. Select the SAUTÉ setting on your Instant Pot and set to More. When the screen says Hot, swirl in the oil. Wait a few seconds and then put in the red chili or chilies. Stir once and then add the garlic. Stir until the pieces turn golden. Now put in all the kale greens and stir until they change color to a brighter green. Add 1 cup water and salt. Hit CANCEL TO reset the cooking program.

3. Close and seal the lid. Cook at LOW PRESSURE for 4 minutes, and then release the pressure manually.

4. Hit CANCEL. Remove the lid, venting any remaining steam away from you. Remove the red chili or chilies and mash the garlic into the greens.

SOUTHERN-STYLE MUSHROOMS IN A CREAMY COCONUT SAUCE

SERVES 4

This dish comes from the southwestern Indian region of Coorg (now called by its original name, Kodagu), where, in the long rainy season, wild mushrooms of every variety grow abundantly in the forests. This recipe, however, is made with the small white button mushrooms that you can find in supermarkets. It is generally served with rice. You may also serve it with rice noodles, which are made quite commonly in most Coorg households but that you will have to get in their dry form—rice sticks—from East Asian markets. You could also serve this with noodles or Italian vermicelli or spaghettini.

Leave your can of coconut milk standing still, with the top up, for twenty-four hours. Just before using, open the can carefully without tilting it too much. Now spoon off the very thick creamy coconut milk that has risen to the top and put it in a bowl. This is the thick coconut milk. What remains in the can is the thin coconut milk.

One 14-ounce can unsweetened coconut milk (see headnote)

1 pound small white button mushrooms

1 teaspoon salt, or to taste

¼ teaspoon ground turmeric

4 tablespoons peanut or olive oil

6 tablespoons peeled and very finely chopped shallots

2 teaspoons ground coriander

¼–½ teaspoon chili powder

1–3 fresh hot green chilies (such as bird's-eye), finely chopped

1 tablespoon lime juice

1. Divide the coconut milk into thick and thin coconut milk as suggested in the headnote.

2. Wipe off the mushrooms with a damp paper towel and cut each in half. Larger mushrooms may be quartered. Put all the mushroom pieces in a bowl and sprinkle the salt and turmeric over them. Wearing plastic gloves if you wish, as turmeric can stain, rub these flavorings into the mushrooms. Set aside for 10 minutes.

3. Select the SAUTÉ setting on your Instant Pot and set to More. When the screen says Hot, swirl in the oil. Add the shallots. Stir and fry until they just start to brown, about 2–3 minutes. Add the coriander and chili powder, stir a few times, then add the green chilies. Stir a few times. Add the mushrooms and all the accumulated liquid in

the bowl. Stir and cook for 2 minutes. Now add
¾ cup of the thin coconut milk and stir it in. Hit
CANCEL to reset the cooking program. Close and
seal the lid and cook at LOW PRESSURE, setting
the timer for 1 minute. As soon as the screen
says 1, hit CANCEL and reduce the pressure
manually. Remove the lid carefully, venting the
remaining steam away from you.

4. Select the SAUTÉ setting and set to Normal.
Add ¼ cup of the thick coconut milk and stir
it in. Cook for another 2 minutes, stirring now
and then. Add the lime juice and stir it in. Hit
CANCEL or KEEP WARM, as desired.

POTATOES IN A MARWARI STYLE

SERVES 3–4

Marwaris are a community that originated in the deserts of Rajasthan but are now scattered all over India. Their business is money, and they are traditionally vegetarian. Some are as rich as Croesus, others have a little less. But their food, whether in very wealthy households or mere middle-class ones, is almost uniformly superb. Generally spicy and rich, it exists in a class by itself.

These potatoes are nearly always served with Indian breads as part of a meal that could include a dish of peas, carrots, or spinach, a dal, and a yogurt relish.

4 large red potatoes, peeled and quartered into large chunky pieces

¾ teaspoon salt, or to taste

¼ teaspoon ground turmeric

⅛–½ teaspoon chili powder

1 teaspoon ground coriander

4 tablespoons peanut or olive oil

⅛ teaspoon ground asafetida

¼ teaspoon whole cumin seeds

1 dried hot red chili, broken in half

½ medium onion, thinly sliced into half-rings

1½ teaspoons fresh peeled ginger grated to a pulp

1 fresh hot green chili (like bird's-eye), thinly sliced into rounds

2 tablespoons chopped cilantro leaves

1. Pour 1 cup water into the Instant Pot and set a steaming basket or trivet on top of it. Lay all the potatoes in the basket or on top of the trivet. Close and seal the lid. Select the **STEAM** setting set to low pressure, setting the timer for 3 minutes. When the 3 minutes are over, release the steam manually and hit **CANCEL** to reset the cooking program. Remove the lid, venting the remaining steam away from you. Weaing oven mitts, lift out the basket or trivet and set down to cool. Meanwhile, clean the inner pot and dry it thoroughly inside and out. Put it back in the outer pot.

2. When the potatoes have cooled down, put them in a wide, shallow bowl. Sprinkle the salt, turmeric, chili powder, and coriander over the top and mix gently but thoroughly.

3. Select the **SAUTÉ** setting on your Instant Pot and set to More, setting the timer for 30 minutes. When the screen says Hot, swirl in the oil. Add the asafetida, cumin seeds, and broken red chili. Let them sizzle for a few seconds. Stir

once, turning the chili pieces over. Now put in all the onions and stir once or twice. Put in the ginger and green chilies. Stir for a minute, then add all the potatoes. Cook for another 7–8 minutes, stirring carefully so as not to break the potato pieces and gently scraping from the bottom until the potatoes have browned a bit and are encrusted with the spices. Check the salt. This dish is best served while the potatoes are still hot and crisp with the cilantro sprinkled over the top.

SPICY FAT FRENCH FRIES

SERVES 3–4

I do not deep-fry here. Instead, I use the Instant Pot and my oven to achieve the same delicious results.

You may serve these fries as a snack with ketchup or do as I do: Make the Easy Tamarind Chutney (page 142), then swirl in 2 tablespoons of beaten plain yogurt so you see both the brown and the white colors, and use this as a dip. Put the fries and the chutney conveniently on a table in front of the TV. Get a few napkins to wipe your hands. Now, tuck in. Dip and eat as you watch your favorite TV show!

4 large red potatoes, about 1¾ pounds

3 tablespoons peanut or olive oil

¾ teaspoon salt, or to taste

¼ teaspoon ground turmeric

⅛–½ teaspoon chili powder

1 teaspoon ground cumin

1 teaspoon ground coriander

Freshly ground black pepper

1. Peel the potatoes and keep them in a bowl of water as you cut them. Cut each potato in half lengthways, along its slimmer side. Now cut each half in thirds lengthways, to make fat fries. Keep in the bowl of water.

2. Pour 1 cup water into the Instant Pot and set a steaming basket or trivet on top of it. Lift the potatoes out of the bowl of water and lay them down in the basket or on top of the trivet. Place the cover on top of the pot. Close and seal the lid. Select the STEAM setting and set to low pressure, setting the time at 3 minutes. When the 3 minutes are over, release the steam manually. Hit CANCEL to reset the cooking program. Remove the lid, venting the steam away from you. Lift out the basket or trivet with oven mitts and set down to cool.

3. Preheat the oven to 500°F.

4. When the potatoes have cooled off completely, spread them out in a large, wide bowl. Pour

the oil over them and rub it on evenly. Now sprinkle the salt, turmeric, chili powder, cumin, coriander, and black pepper over the top and mix it in as evenly as you can.

5. Spread the fries out on a nonstick baking tray in a single layer. Place in the top third of the oven for 10 minutes or until one side is lightly browned. Turn the fries over and bake another 10 minutes or so, until the second side is also lightly browned. Serve immediately.

SOUTH INDIAN MIXED-VEGETABLE KORMA

SERVES 4

This all-vegetarian curry has a sauce that is made with a mixture of cashews, tomatoes, and coconut. It is utterly delicious and may be eaten with rice, or better still, served over rice noodles. South Indian rice noodles are very thin and made at home with a special gadget. To substitute, you may use Vietnamese *banh pho,* which are sold in their dried form by most East Asian grocers. A recipe on how to cook them is on page 149.

2 tablespoons chopped raw cashews

3 medium tomatoes, peeled and chopped (canned will do)

¾–1 teaspoon salt

1–4 fresh hot green chilies (such as bird's-eye)

½ teaspoon My Garam Masala (page 154)

4 tablespoons chopped cilantro

2 tablespoons peanut or olive oil

½ teaspoon whole brown or black mustard seeds

1 teaspoon urad dal or yellow split peas

10 fresh curry leaves, if available

1 cup peeled carrots cut into ½-inch rounds

1 cup peas, fresh or defrosted frozen

1 cup ¾-inch cauliflower florets

1 cup green beans trimmed and cut into ¾-inch lengths

½ cup coconut milk from a well-shaken can

1. Cover the cashews in hot water and soak for 1 hour. Drain.

2. Put the cashews, tomatoes, ½ teaspoon salt, chili or chilies, and garam masala into a blender. Blend until you have a smooth paste. Add the cilantro and blend for just a second, as you want flecks of green in the sauce.

3. Select the SAUTÉ setting on your Instant Pot and set to More. When the screen says Hot, swirl in the oil. Wait a few seconds, then put in the mustard seeds and the urad dal. Stir until the urad dal turns reddish. Add the curry leaves.

They will splatter, so stand back. Quickly put in carrots, peas, cauliflower, green beans, and ¼ teaspoon salt. Stir a few times and add 1 cup water. Hit CANCEL to reset the cooking program.

4. Close and seal the lid. Cook on LOW PRESSURE, setting the timer for 1 minute. When the cooking time is up, release the pressure manually. Hit CANCEL and open the pot, venting the remaining steam away from you. Stir to mix. Select the SAUTÉ setting and set to Normal. Add the coconut milk and stir it in. Check the salt. You might want to add a bit more. Cook gently for another minute. Hit CANCEL or KEEP WARM as desired.

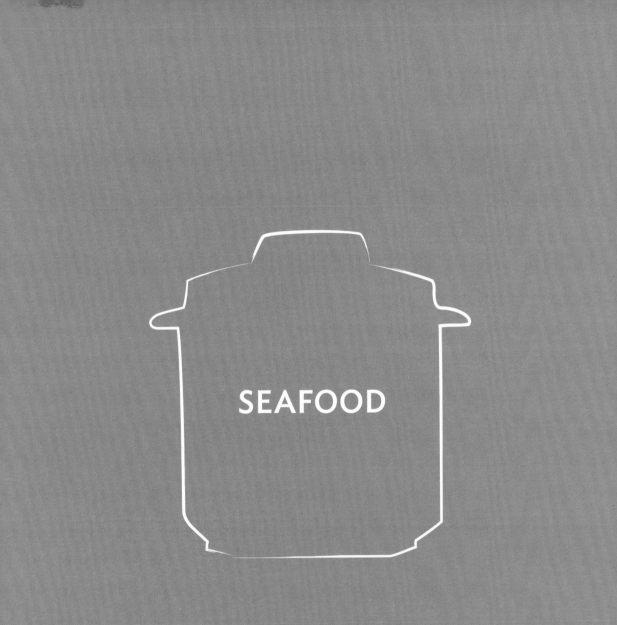

SEAFOOD

FENNEL-FLAVORED FISH CURRY WITH CAULIFLOWER

SERVES 3–4

Many different types of firm-fleshed seafood could be used to make this highly flavored, spicy dish: salmon, halibut, kingfish, and shrimp would be ideal, and haddock and cod may be used with some care. I generally use halibut filet and it turns out beautifully.

For the cauliflower, I buy a large head and break off four of the large florets on the outside edge. I cut these in halves lengthways, through the stem. The pieces need to be chunky to keep their shape.

This is best served with rice, but small pasta, like orzo, would also be wonderful.

FOR MARINATING THE FISH

1⅓–1½ pounds fish as
    suggested in headnote,
    with skin removed
¼ teaspoon salt
¼ teaspoon chili powder
¼ teaspoon ground turmeric

FOR THE POACHING SAUCE

1 tablespoon ground coriander
1 teaspoon ground cumin
¼ teaspoon ground turmeric
¼–½ teaspoon chili powder
2 teaspoons hot curry powder
    (I like Bolst's)
½ teaspoon salt (plus
    ⅛ teaspoon for the
    cauliflower)
1 cup peeled and finely
    chopped tomatoes, fresh
    or canned
3 tablespoons peanut or olive
    oil

FOR THE POACHING SAUCE *continued*

½ teaspoon whole black or
    brown mustard seeds
1 teaspoon fennel seeds
4 very large cauliflower florets,
    halved lengthways
    (see headnote)

1. To marinate the fish: If the fish is a chunky, center-cut filet, cut it into roughly 2-inch squares. If using shrimp, just peel and devein. Rub with the marinade seasonings: salt, chili powder, and turmeric. Cover and refrigerate while you prepare the sauce.

2. To prepare the poaching sauce: Put the coriander, cumin, turmeric, chili powder, curry powder, salt, tomatoes, and ¾ cup water into a small bowl. Mix thoroughly.

3. Select the SAUTÉ setting on your Instant Pot and set to More. When the screen says Hot, add oil, put in the mustard seeds and the fennel

seeds. Stir a few times. Put in the cauliflower florets. Stir them around until they are brown in spots. Sprinkle ⅛ teaspoon salt over them and stir for another minute. Now pour in the sauce and stir. Press CANCEL to reset the cooking program.

4. Cover and seal the lid. Cook at LOW PRESSURE for 2 minutes. Release the pressure manually. Remove the lid, venting the remaining steam away from you.

5. Select the SAUTÉ setting and set to Normal. Remove the cauliflower florets with a slotted spoon and save on a plate. Put all the fish pieces into the sauce in a single layer. Spoon sauce over the fish as it poaches. When the undersides have turned opaque, carefully turn the pieces over. When the second side is done (the poaching takes just a few minutes), put the cauliflower back in and heat through.

GOAN SHRIMP CURRY

Samar Codi

SERVES 4

This is the hot "prawn curry," as it is called here, found on the beaches of Goa. It is very simple to prepare, and is delicious eaten with rice. Normally, several teaspoons of a very red but milder chili powder would be used here. I have suggested less and used paprika to add to the color.

½–1 teaspoon chili powder

1 tablespoon bright red paprika

½ teaspoon ground turmeric

4 cloves garlic, peeled and crushed to a pulp

2 teaspoons peeled fresh ginger grated to a pulp

2 tablespoons ground coriander

1 teaspoon ground cumin

¾ teaspoon salt, or to taste

2 teaspoons tamarind paste, or to taste (use lemon juice to taste as a substitute)

1 pound medium shrimp, peeled and deveined

1 cup coconut milk from a well-stirred can

1. Put the chili powder, paprika, turmeric, garlic, ginger, coriander, and cumin in a bowl. Slowly add 1¼ cups water, mixing as you go. Pour this mixture into the inner pot of your Instant Pot. Close and seal the lid. Cook at **LOW PRESSURE** for 5 minutes and let the pressure drop by itself for 10 minutes. Release the remaining pressure manually. Open the lid, venting the remaining steam away from you.

2. Add the salt and tamarind or lemon juice to the sauce, balancing the flavors to your taste. The sauce will seem a bit rough at this stage. Select the **SAUTÉ** setting set to Normal. Add the shrimp and the coconut milk. Stir gently and cook until all the shrimp have turned opaque. Taste the sauce again for balance of flavors.

SHRIMP STEAMED WITH MUSTARD

Bhapay Jhinga
SERVES 4

This dish, simplified from its Bengali version, which uses freshly ground mustard seeds, may be eaten hot with rice, the Bengali way, or the shrimp, with their little bit of sauce, could be divided up between old-fashioned soup plates and served topped with baby arugula or young chrysanthemum leaves in a lemony dressing. If you use mustard oil in the cooking, you could use a little mustard oil in the dressing as well. (See page 136 for Baby Arugula Salad with Mustard Oil.) This way you have a modern dish with ancient roots.

1 pound large shrimp, peeled and deveined (about 20; fresh shrimp, if you can get them, are ideal)

A scant ½ teaspoon salt

¼ teaspoon ground turmeric

½ teaspoon ground coriander

½ teaspoon ground roasted cumin seeds (page 152)

¼–½ teaspoon chili powder

1 tablespoon mustard powder (like Colman's)

1 fresh green bird's-eye chili, chopped (optional)

1 tablespoon mustard oil or extra-virgin olive oil

1. Put the shrimp in a bowl. Add the salt, turmeric, coriander, cumin, chili powder, and mustard powder. Mix well. Add the green chili, if using, 1 cup water, and the oil. Mix again. Put the shrimp and all the juices into the shallowest heatproof bowl that can fit inside the inner pot of your Instant Pot.

2. Put the Instant Pot steaming rack in position. Place a large sling made out of foil on the rack, making sure that it is long enough to come high up both sides of the bowl. (For further directions, see page xii of the introduction.) Pour 1 cup water into the inner pot and set the bowl with the shrimp on top of the steaming rack. Lock and seal the lid. Select STEAM and set to low pressure, setting the timer for 2 minutes. When the cooking is done, release the pressure manually. Open the lid carefully, venting the remaining steam away from you. Wearing oven mitts, stir the shrimp. Cover with the lid once again, locking and sealing it. Select the STEAM setting and cook at low pressure for another 2 minutes. Release the steam manually. Open the lid carefully, venting the remaining steam away from you, and remove the shrimp bowl with the help of the sling.

KERALA SHRIMP WITH COCONUT MILK

Konju Pappas

SERVES 6

This is one of coastal India's finest shrimp dishes. Almost everything in it was local for the lady in Kerala who first cooked it for me. Most of the spices and coconuts grew in her garden. As for the shrimp, they came from the ocean that laps the shores of her state just a boat ride away.

This dish is always served with rice. In Kerala it could be Plain Brown or Red Basmati Rice (page 118), or a short-grained rice akin to jasmine rice.

2 tablespoons whole coriander seeds

¼ teaspoon whole fenugreek seeds

1 teaspoon whole black peppercorns

3 tablespoons vegetable oil

1 teaspoon whole black mustard seeds

10 fresh curry leaves, if available

1 medium onion, cut into fine half-rings

4 cloves garlic, peeled and cut into fine slivers

1 teaspoon peeled fresh ginger grated to a pulp

2 tablespoons bright red paprika

¾ teaspoon chili powder

½ teaspoon ground turmeric

¾–1 teaspoon salt

2–3 teaspoons tamarind paste

1¾ cups canned or frozen coconut milk

2 pounds medium shrimp, peeled and deveined

1–3 fresh slim green chilies

1. Set a small cast-iron frying pan on medium heat. When hot, put in the coriander and fenugreek seeds and the peppercorns. Stir them around for about a minute or until they seem toasted. Remove from the heat and empty the pan onto a clean paper towel. Let the spices cool off. Then grind them finely in a clean coffee grinder.

2. Select the SAUTÉ setting on your Instant Pot and set to More. When the screen says Hot, put in the oil. Wait a few seconds and then put in the mustard seeds. Stir once or twice and throw in the curry leaves. They will splatter, so stand back. Then add the onions and garlic. Stir and fry until they are lightly browned. Add the ginger and

stir a few times. Then put in 1¼ cups water, the paprika, chili powder, turmeric, salt, tamarind paste, and all the spices from the grinder. Stir to mix. Hit CANCEL to stop the cooking process.

3. Close and seal the lid. Cook at LOW PRESSURE for 2 minutes and then release the pressure manually. Remove the lid, venting the remaining steam away from you.

4. You can hold this sauce for hours in the pot (or for days in the refrigerator). When you are ready to eat, select the SAUTÉ setting and set to Normal. Add the coconut milk and stir until it has heated up. Add all the shrimp. Stir them gently in the sauce, until they just turn opaque all the way through. Cut slits along the lengths of the green chilies and float them on the top.

GOAN-STYLE CLAMS

Thisra

SERVES 2–4

There is nothing quite as exhilarating as sitting on the beach in Goa, ladling these clams and their exquisite juices over rice and then devouring them as the palm trees fan you with their balmy breezes. The little fish shacks in Goa often use tiny cockles, but littleneck clams work equally well.

These days, fishmongers in America usually sell very clean clams that just need to be rinsed out, but if they are muddy, do scrub them with a brush under cold water and then wash them out.

2 teaspoons ground coriander

2 teaspoons ground cumin

¼ teaspoon chili powder

½ teaspoon ground turmeric

1 teaspoon powdered mustard

3 tablespoons peanut or olive oil

⅛ teaspoon whole fenugreek seeds

1¼ cup chopped onions (about ¼-inch pieces)

2 teaspoons peeled fresh ginger grated to a pulp

4 cloves garlic, peeled and crushed to a pulp

1–2 fresh hot green chilies, such as bird's-eye, finely chopped

½ teaspoon salt

24 littleneck clams, cleaned as suggested in headnote

¾ cup coconut milk from a well-shaken can

1. Combine the coriander, cumin, chili powder, turmeric, and mustard in a small bowl.

2. Select the SAUTÉ setting on your Instant Pot and set to More for 30 minutes. When the screen says Hot, put in the fenugreek seeds. Stir a few times. Put in the onions. Stir and cook 3–4 minutes, until the onions are soft and have just begin to darken. Add the ginger, garlic, and green chilies. Stir for a minute. Add all the spices from the small bowl. Stir a few times. Quickly put in 1½ cups water and the salt. Stir, scraping

up anything stuck to the bottom. Hit CANCEL to reset the cooking program.

3. Lock and seal the lid. Cook on LOW PRESSURE for 3 minutes and then let the pressure drop by itself for 10 minutes. If any pressure is left, release it manually. Remove the lid.

4. Select the SAUTÉ setting and set to MORE for 20 minutes. As soon as the sauce starts to bubble, gently put in all the clams. Cover with the glass lid, turn the SAUTÉ function to Normal, and simmer for about 5 minutes or until all the clams open. Remove the glass lid. Add the coconut milk and stir it in. Cook another minute to blend flavors. Hit CANCEL.

HALIBUT OR SALMON IN A GREEN PARSI SAUCE

Parsi Macchi

SERVES 4

For this specialty, served at most Parsi weddings and banquets, a wonderfully meaty flatfish—the pomfret—is smothered in a spicy green chutney, wrapped in a banana leaf, and steamed. In the West, where most people are lucky if they even get frozen banana leaves, aluminum foil is often used as a substitute. Here, to make matters simple, I dispense with the wrapping altogether, adding some tomatoes and onions, which I cook under low pressure to soften them up, and then just poaching the fish in the sauce. It works beautifully. Serve with Saffron Rice with Golden Raisins (page 123) and perhaps Carrots and Peas with Sesame Seeds (page 38).

FOR THE DRY MARINADE FOR THE FISH

1⅓–1½ pounds center-cut halibut filet or salmon filet, with skin removed, cut into roughly 2-by-1-inch pieces

½ teaspoon salt

Lots of freshly ground pepper

¼ teaspoon ground turmeric

¼ teaspoon chili powder

FOR THE GREEN SAUCE

1 well-packed cup mint leaves

2 well-packed cups cilantro leaves and small stems

One 1-inch piece of peeled fresh ginger, finely chopped

1–3 fresh hot green chilies (such as bird's eye), chopped

1 teaspoon ground cumin

⅛–½ teaspoon chili powder

FOR THE GREEN SAUCE *continued*

2 teaspoons sugar

¾ teaspoon salt

3½ tablespoons lemon juice

1 cup coconut milk from a well-shaken can

YOU WILL ALSO NEED

3 tablespoons peanut or olive oil

¼ teaspoon mustard seeds

6 tablespoons finely chopped shallots or onions

2 cloves garlic, peeled and crushed to a pulp

½ cup peeled and finely chopped tomatoes (from a can will do)

A sprinkling of salt

1. To prepare the fish: Rub the fish pieces evenly on both sides with the dry marinade seasonings. Set aside, covered, in the refrigerator for a minimum of 30 minutes and up to 10 hours.

2. To make the sauce: Put 1 cup water, the mint, cilantro, ginger, green chilies, cumin, chili powder, sugar, salt, and lemon juice into a blender. Blend until you have a smooth paste. Add the coconut milk and give the blender another whirr. Pour this paste into a bowl. Add another ½ cup water to the blender. Slosh around to pick up any remaining sauce and add to the sauce in the bowl. Taste for balance of flavors.

3. Select the SAUTÉ setting on your Instant Pot and set to More. When the screen says Hot, swirl in the oil. A few seconds later, add the mustard seeds. As soon as they pop, put in the shallots. Stir and fry for 2–3 minutes or until they just start to brown. Add the garlic and stir once or twice. Add the tomatoes and stir until the mixture thickens. Add a sprinkling of salt and ½ cup water. Hit CANCEL to reset the cooking program.

4. Close and seal the lid. Cook on LOW PRESSURE for 1 minute and then release the pressure manually. Take off the lid carefully, venting the remaining steam away from you. Stir the tomato sauce in the pot and slowly add the green sauce from the bowl. Select the SAUTÉ setting and set to Normal. When the sauce starts simmering, slip the fish pieces into the pot in a single layer. Poach the fish for 2 minutes, spooning the sauce gently over it as it cooks. Turn the fish pieces over carefully and poach another 3–4 minutes or until the fish is cooked through.

SALMON IN A BENGALI MUSTARD SAUCE

Bangali Macchi
SERVES 4

Bengalis use freshly ground mustard seeds to make the sauce for this dish but I often make matters easier for myself by just using Colman's mustard powder. Serve with plain basmati rice (to soak up all the juices), a dal, and a green vegetable. Don't be afraid to serve it sometimes in an American way, with boiled baby potatoes and a vegetable, such as spinach, if you wish. Bengalis tend to make this dish quite hot. You can decide for yourself.

FOR THE DRY MARINADE FOR THE FISH
1⅓–1½ pounds center-cut salmon filet, with the skin removed, and cut into roughly 2-by-1-inch pieces
½ teaspoon salt
Lots of freshly ground pepper
¼ teaspoon ground turmeric
¼ teaspoon chili powder

FOR THE SAUCE
6 tablespoons mustard powder (see headnote)
¼–½ teaspoon chili powder
¼ teaspoon ground turmeric
½ teaspoon salt
2 tablespoons mustard oil (you can use extra-virgin olive oil as a substitute)
¼ teaspoon whole mustard seeds
¼ teaspoon whole cumin seeds

FOR THE SAUCE *continued*
¼ teaspoon fennel seeds
¼ teaspoon nigella
1–2 fresh hot green bird's-eye chilies, slit slightly in the middle

1. To prepare the fish: Rub the fish pieces evenly on both sides with the dry marinade seasonings. Set aside, covered, in the refrigerator for a minimum of 30 minutes and up to 10 hours.

2. To make the sauce: Put the mustard powder, chili powder, turmeric, and salt in a small bowl. Very slowly add ½ cup water, mixing with a small whisk as you go to make a lump-free paste. Now add 1½ cups more water and whisk it in. Set aside.

3. Select the SAUTÉ setting on your Instant Pot and set to More. Pour in the mustard oil. When the screen says Hot, put in the mustard, cumin, and fennel seeds, and the nigella. Stir until you

hear the mustard seeds pop, then quickly stir the liquid mustard mixture and pour it in. Add the green chilies. Hit CANCEL to reset the cooking program.

4. Lay the fish pieces in the mustard sauce in a single layer and spoon some of the sauce over them. Close and seal the lid. Cook at LOW PRESSURE for 1 minute, then let the pressure release naturally for 5 minutes. Release the rest of the pressure manually. Open the lid carefully, venting the remaining steam away from you.

SQUID IN A TOMATO-CHILI SAUCE

SERVES 4–6

I love squid. These days we can get it already cleaned, so all we have to do is cut it up the way we like. I like squid that are medium sized, with about five-inch-long bodies. Squid is tender and at its best if you either cook it very quickly or cook it for a long time. I have chosen the quick route here. However, the sauce takes a bit longer. This may be served over rice—or, strangely enough, it is wonderful with pasta. I just had it over penne, and it was perfect. Try it.

For the tomatoes needed here, I get a 1¾-pound can of plum tomatoes in tomato puree. I pull out about eight tomatoes and crush them well with my hands in a bowl, enough to get two cups, and save the rest of the can for future use.

3 tablespoons peanut or olive oil

1 teaspoon whole black or brown mustard seeds

2–3 dried hot red chilies

10–15 fresh curry leaves

1 tablespoon peeled fresh ginger grated to a pulp

4 cloves garlic, peeled and crushed

1 teaspoon ground cumin

1 teaspoon ground coriander

2 cups crushed tomatoes (see headnote)

1¼ teaspoons salt

1 pound cleaned squid, with the bodies cut into ¼-inch rings, and the heads halved lengthways

3 tablespoons chopped cilantro

1. Select the **SAUTÉ** setting on your Instant Pot and set to More. When the screen says Hot, swirl in the oil. After a few seconds, put in the mustard seeds and whole chilies. Stir a few times. Add the curry leaves. They will splatter, so stand back. Quickly put in the ginger and garlic. Stir a few times. Add the cumin and coriander. Stir once and add the tomatoes and ¾ teaspoon salt. Stir to mix. Hit **CANCEL** to reset the cooking program. Close and seal the lid. Cook at **LOW PRESSURE** for 3 minutes and then let the pressure release naturally for 5 minutes. Release the rest of the pressure manually. Hit **CANCEL**.

2. Take the lid off, venting the steam away from you. Stir the sauce and remove the whole chilies. Select the **SAUTÉ** setting and set to Normal. Put all the squid and the remaining ½ teaspoon salt into the pot. Stir gently and cook just until all the squid turns opaque, a matter of a minute or two. Wearing oven mitts, lift the inner pot out of the outer pot and set it aside to stop any further cooking. Add the cilantro before serving.

POULTRY
AND EGGS

PRESSURE-COOKED EGGS

The Instant Pot is so good for boiling eggs, not because it saves time but because it makes peeling them so much easier. I also find it very convenient, especially when I need large numbers. (See Eggs in a Tomato-Tamarind Hyderabadi Sauce, page 75.) Some people cook at high pressure, some at low pressure. I prefer the low-pressure method.

I put all the eggs I want to cook in a steaming basket, but if you do not have one, just pile them up gently on the steaming rack and then lift them out carefully one by one with tongs. Soft-boiled eggs will take about 5 minutes and hard-boiled eggs about 8 minutes. If you want your yolks semi-hard, you will have to play around with 6–7 minutes, all at low pressure. The size of the eggs will also make a slight difference in the timing. These timings work for large eggs. I happen to get my eggs at a farm where eggs come in all sizes and colors. After a little trial and error, you will get exactly the kind of eggs you want.

Note: If you leave the eggs in the ice water for just 2 minutes and then remove and peel them, they will still be warm inside. Leave them longer if you want them completely chilled.

1. Prepare a large bowl of ice water.

2. Place your eggs carefully in a steaming basket and lower it into the inner container of the Instant Pot. Add 1 cup water. (If you do not have a basket, set your trivet inside the inner container. Add 1 cup of water and put all the eggs you want to cook carefully on the trivet, in a pyramid form, if needed.)

3. Close and seal the lid. Cook at LOW PRESSURE for 5 minutes for soft-boiled eggs and 8 minutes for hard-boiled eggs. Release the pressure manually. Remove the lid carefully, venting the remaining steam away from you. Lift out the basket and lower it into the bowl of ice water. (If you are using a trivet, you will have to use tongs to pick up the eggs one by one and quickly and carefully lower them into the ice water.)

EGGS IN A TOMATO-TAMARIND HYDERABADI SAUCE

Timatar Kut

SERVES 3–4

This recipe is a specialty of the Hyderabad region of southern India, where conquering Muslim rulers from the north soon succumbed to the Hindu spicing traditions of their subjects. Their royal food became a glorious blend of the Delhi Mughal court and local dishes.

Here hard-boiled eggs are served in a tomato sauce seasoned with tamarind, mustard seeds, curry leaves, and fenugreek seeds, the seasonings all very much a part of the South Indian, Hindu culinary tradition. Of course, tomatoes originated in the New World and were brought into India by the Portuguese—but that is another story!

Serve with rice or flatbreads. You may serve these eggs at all meals, from breakfast to dinner.

FOR THE SAUCE

2 cups tomato puree (or strained tomatoes or passata)

1 tablespoon ground coriander

4–5 teaspoons tamarind paste, or to taste (you can use 1 tablespoon lemon juice as a substitute)

2 teaspoons peeled fresh ginger grated to a pulp

1 clove garlic, peeled and crushed to a pulp

¼–½ teaspoon chili powder

2 tablespoons cilantro leaves, chopped

1 teaspoon ground roasted cumin seeds (page 152)

1¼ teaspoons salt, or to taste

YOU WILL ALSO NEED

2 teaspoons chickpea flour

¼ teaspoon whole black mustard seeds

¼ teaspoon whole cumin seeds

¼ teaspoon nigella (kalonji in Indian stores)

⅛ teaspoon whole fenugreek seeds

2 dried hot red chilies

1 clove garlic, peeled and cut into quarters lengthways

2 tablespoons peanut or olive oil

10 fresh curry leaves, if available

6 hard-boiled eggs (page 74), peeled and cut into halves lengthways

1. Put the tomato puree in a bowl. Add all the other ingredients for the sauce and mix well. Taste for balance of flavors and make adjustments, if needed.

2. Put a small cast-iron skillet on medium heat. When hot, put in the chickpea flour. Stir it around until it turns a shade darker, a matter of minutes, and remove to a small bowl. Slowly add 2 tablespoons water, first making a smooth paste with just a little water and then adding the rest. Set aside.

3. Put the mustard seeds, cumin seeds, nigella, fenugreek, red chilies, and garlic in a small bowl. Set aside.

4. Select the SAUTÉ setting on your Instant Pot and set to More for 30 minutes. When the screen says Hot, add oil, put in all the spices from the small bowl. Stir until the garlic turns golden. Add the curry leaves. They will splatter, so stand back. Stir once and then pour in all the tomato mixture. Stir once and hit CANCEL to reset the cooking program.

5. Close and seal the lid. Cook at LOW PRESSURE for 1 minute. Release the pressure manually. Open the lid, venting the remaining steam away from you. Stir the sauce. Select the SAUTÉ setting and set to Normal. Stir the chickpea flour mixture and pour it in. Stir gently until the sauce thickens a bit, 2–3 minutes. Hit CANCEL. Wearing oven mitts, lift out the inner pot to stop the cooking. Taste for salt.

To serve, put the sauce in a shallow serving dish, arranging the egg halves on top.

GROUND TURKEY WITH POTATOES

Keema Aloo

SERVES 3–4

This delightful, everyday meat-and-potato dish is usually made with ground lamb or goat meat in India, but I often make it with turkey, especially when my husband and I are trying to take a break from red meat. (*Keema* means "ground meat.") I prefer ground turkey that has both the dark and light meat mixed together—just white meat makes the keema too dry. We both love the dish, and sometimes when we are rushed we just serve it with a big salad. When we want a full Indian meal, we serve it with a dal (Mung Dal with Spinach, on page 18, would complement it well), a yogurt relish, and either some rice or an Indian flatbread.

FOR THE POTATOES

3 large red potatoes (about 1 pound or a bit less), peeled and cut into 6–8 chunky pieces each

1 teaspoon peanut or olive oil

¼ teaspoon salt

¼ teaspoon ground turmeric

⅛ teaspoon chili powder

¼ teaspoon nice red paprika

FOR THE KEEMA

3 tablespoons peanut or olive oil

1 medium cinnamon stick

1 bay leaf

1 medium onion, chopped

2 teaspoons peeled fresh ginger grated to a pulp

3 cloves garlic, peeled and crushed to a pulp

FOR THE KEEMA *continued*

2 teaspoons ground coriander

1 teaspoon ground cumin

½ teaspoon ground turmeric

¼–½ teaspoon chili powder

½ teaspoon nice red paprika

1 pound ground turkey

4 tablespoons plain yogurt, the sourer, the better

2 medium tomatoes, peeled and finely chopped (canned will do)

1 teaspoon salt

Cilantro leaves and/or green chilies of your choosing (chopped or whole), for garnishing (optional)

1. Put the potato pieces in a bowl and rub with the oil. Sprinkle the listed seasonings over them and mix well. Set aside.

2. Select the SAUTÉ setting on your Instant Pot and set to More for 30 minutes. When the display says Hot, swirl in the oil. Wait a few seconds and put in the cinnamon sick and bay leaf. Stir a few times, add the onions, and stir and cook for 3–4 minutes or until the onions brown a little. Add the ginger and garlic, stir a few times, then add the coriander, cumin, turmeric, chili powder, and paprika. Stir once or twice. Add the ground turkey. Stir and cook, breaking up all lumps and scraping from the bottom at the same time. Begin to add the yogurt, 1 tablespoon at a time, as you continue to stir and break up lumps into ever-smaller pieces and stir from the bottom. Now add the tomatoes and salt. Mix well, again scraping from the bottom. Add 1 cup water and hit CANCEL to reset the cooking program.

3. Close and seal the lid. Cook at LOW PRESSURE for 6 minutes. Release the steam manually and remove the lid carefully, venting the remaining steam away from you. Empty the bowl of potatoes over the meat, spreading them evenly over the top. Put the lid back on and reseal it. Cook at LOW PRESSURE for 5 minutes and then release the steam manually. Hit CANCEL and remove the lid carefully, venting it away from you. Garnish when serving, if desired.

BUTTER CHICKEN

Murgh Makkhani

SERVES 4–6

While I was a youngster in Delhi, just after India's partition, refugees from the Punjab opened the first tandoori restaurant there. They offered tandoori chicken and naan (slightly raised flatbreads), which thrilled us all, but they also served this Butter Chicken. They just took freshly cooked tandoori chicken, cut it into smaller sections, and then smothered it in a tomato-cream sauce to which they also added butter at the very end. It was rich and glorious. Here is my Instant Pot version of the same dish.

FOR THE MARINADE

¼ cup plain yogurt

¾ teaspoon salt

½ cup chopped onions

One 1-inch piece of peeled fresh ginger, finely chopped

½–1 fresh hot green chili, chopped (optional)

⅛–½ teaspoon chili powder

1 teaspoon My Garam Masala (page 154)

1½ tablespoons lemon juice

1½ pounds boneless, skinless chicken thighs, cut into roughly 1½–2-inch squares

FOR THE SAUCE

1¼ cups tomato puree (or passata or strained tomatoes)

1 teaspoon peeled fresh ginger grated to a pulp

1 teaspoon salt

FOR THE SAUCE *continued*

½–1 fresh hot green chili, finely chopped (optional)

⅛–½ teaspoon chili powder

4 teaspoons lemon juice

1 teaspoon ground roasted cumin seeds (page 152), plus more for garnishing

½ teaspoon My Garam Masala (page 154)

YOU WILL ALSO NEED

About 5 tablespoons peanut or olive oil

¾ cup heavy cream

1 tablespoon unsalted butter, cut into smaller pats

Cilantro leaves, for garnishing

1. To make the marinade for the chicken: Put the yogurt, salt, onions, ginger, green chilies, if using, chili powder, garam masala, and lemon juice into a blender. Blend until smooth. Put all

the chicken pieces in a bowl. Pour the marinade over the top. Prick the chicken pieces with the tip of a knife and mix well. Cover and marinate overnight in the refrigerator (or for at least 4 hours).

2. To make the sauce (just before you cook): Combine the tomato puree, ginger, salt, green chilies, if using, chili powder, lemon juice, cumin seeds, and garam masala in a bowl. Stir to mix well.

3. Select the SAUTÉ setting on your Instant Pot and set to More for 30 minutes. Lift the chicken pieces out of the bowl they were marinating in, leaving most of the marinade behind. When the screen says Hot, swirl in 3 tablespoons of the oil. Wait a few seconds and add in 5–6 pieces of chicken wherever you see the oil. Do not try to move them until they have browned, about 1½–2 minutes. Then turn them over and brown the second side. When both sides have browned, remove the chicken pieces and put them in a bowl. Add another 5–6 pieces to the Instant Pot and brown them the same way. After about the third lot, you will need to add another 2 tablespoons of oil. Continue browning the chicken until all the pieces are done.

4. Add ½ cup water to the pot and scrape up all the brown bits stuck to the bottom. Wearing oven mitts, remove the inner pot and discard its contents. You do not need to clean it out thoroughly. Just make sure that the outside is quite dry.

5. Put the inner pot back into the Instant Pot and pour in the tomato puree mixture as well as ¼ cup water. Close and seal the lid. Cook on **LOW PRESSURE** for 1 minute. Release the pressure manually. Open the lid, venting the remaining steam away from you.

6. Select the **SAUTÉ** setting and set to More. Stir the sauce and boil it down slightly to thicken it a bit. Taste for balance of flavors. Adjust the **SAUTÉ** setting to Normal. Add the cream. Stir and bring to a simmer. Add all the chicken and its juices. Stir and cook gently for 2–3 minutes or until the chicken is just cooked through. Press **CANCEL** to reset the cooking program. Just before serving, stir in the butter.

7. Scatter cilantro leaves over the top when serving.

CHICKEN COOKED WITH KERALA'S SEASONINGS

SERVES 4–6

There is a hot, sweet, and sour shrimp dish from Kerala that I love. (Kerala Shrimp with Coconut Milk, page 61.) One day, I started cooking chicken with the same seasonings. I loved that, too. I find it very interesting that centuries before chilies were brought into India via Kerala by Portuguese traders, it was black pepper, a local spice, that provided all the spiciness in the dish. You will find black pepper used in two ways here, both plain and roasted.

Serve with rice—brown, red, or white, according to your preference. It is perfect for sopping up all the good juices. A vegetable or a salad would complete the meal perfectly. In India, we always take the chicken skin off before cooking. I also like to remove the extra fat on the chicken thighs. All Indian stores now sell tamarind paste. I can even find it in specialty stores that are not Indian. Once it is opened, I keep it in the refrigerator. It lasts forever.

8 chicken thighs, about 3¼ pounds, with bone and skin

Salt

Freshly ground pepper

2 tablespoons whole coriander seeds

2 teaspoons whole peppercorns

¼ teaspoon whole fenugreek seeds

5 tablespoons peanut or other oil of your choice

1 teaspoon whole black mustard seeds

15 fresh curry leaves, if available (leave them out if you cannot get fresh ones)

1 large onion, chopped coarsely

One 3-inch piece peeled fresh ginger, grated

5 cloves garlic, peeled and crushed

½ teaspoon ground turmeric

¼–1 teaspoon chili powder

1 tablespoon nice red paprika for color

1 tablespoon tamarind paste

1 cup coconut milk from a well-stirred can

1–3 bird's-eye chilies (if even more heat is desired), with slits cut along their centers lengthways

1. Remove skin and extra fat from the chicken thighs. Salt and pepper them on both sides and set them aside.

2. Put a small cast-iron frying pan over a medium-high flame and let it get hot. Put the coriander seeds, peppercorns, and fenugreek seeds into the pan. Stir the spices until they turn just a shade darker. You will be able to smell the roasted aroma. This happens fast. Empty the spices into a bowl. When cool, grind them in a clean coffee grinder reserved for spices. Put the spices back in the bowl.

3. Select the SAUTÉ setting on your Instant Pot and set to More. When the screen says Hot, swirl in 3 tablespoons of the oil. Wait a few seconds and then put in 4 of the thighs and let them brown lightly on one side, about 3–4 minutes. Do the same on the other side. Remove thighs to a plate. Lightly brown the 4 other thighs the same way and remove to the same plate.

4. Add the remaining 2 tablespoons of oil to the Instant Pot. Allow it to get hot, then put in the mustard seeds. As soon as they pop, a matter of seconds, put in the curry leaves, which will make a splattering sound. Add the chopped onions immediately. Stir and sauté for 2–3 minutes or until the onions are slightly softened. Then add the ginger and garlic and continue to sauté for another 2 minutes. Add 1 cup water and stir, scraping up any browned bits at the bottom. Add the turmeric, chili powder,

paprika, tamarind paste, 1 teaspoon salt, and the roasted spice mixture from the bowl. Stir and mix well. Now put in all the chicken pieces and any accumulated juices as well as 1½ cups water. Press CANCEL to reset the cooking program and close and seal the lid. Set pressure release to Sealing. Cook at LOW PRESSURE for 6 minutes. Hit CANCEL. Perform a quick release by turning the steam release handle on the lid to the Venting position.

5. Hit CANCEL. Open the pot carefully, venting the remaining steam away from you. Select the SAUTÉ setting and set to Less. Cover either with a glass lid or loosely with the regular lid. Let the chicken simmer gently for 7–10 minutes. Stir in the coconut milk and taste for balance of flavors. Add the green chilies, if desired, stir, and let the pot come to a simmer. Cook for another 2 minutes, stirring now and then.

CHICKEN IN A YOGURT SAUCE

SERVES 4–5

This is an excellent dish to make if you are entertaining. Serve it with Saffron Rice with Golden Raisins (page 123). Make the chicken first and remove it from the Instant Pot (it can be reheated later in a microwave oven). Clean out the inner pot, dry it well, and then make the rice.

2 pounds boned and skinned chicken thighs, most blobs of fat removed, cut into 1½-inch pieces

Salt

Freshly ground pepper

1 teaspoon ground cumin

1 teaspoon ground coriander

¼–1 teaspoon chili powder

One 3-inch piece peeled fresh ginger, chopped

4 cloves garlic, peeled and chopped

2 green bird's-eye chilies or ½–1 jalapeño, chopped, with seeds

2 tablespoons chickpea flour

1 cup plain yogurt, the sourer, the better

¾ teaspoon ground turmeric

4 tablespoons peanut or olive oil

15–20 fresh curry leaves, if available

1 cup chopped fresh cilantro leaves

1 teaspoon My Garam Masala (page 154)

1. Sprinkle the chicken pieces evenly on both sides with 1 teaspoon salt, lots of black pepper, the cumin, coriander, and chili powder. Mix well, put in a bowl, cover, and refrigerate overnight if you have the time, or for as little as an hour.

2. Put the ginger, garlic, green chilies, and about 6 tablespoons water into a blender and blend to a paste, pushing down with a rubber spatula as needed. Scrape out the paste and put in a bowl. Set aside.

3. Put the chickpea flour in another bowl. Slowly add 1 cup water, a teaspoon at a time, mixing with a whisk until you have a very smooth, lumpless paste. Now whisk in the yogurt, turmeric, and ½ teaspoon salt. Set aside.

Select the SAUTÉ setting on your Instant Pot and set to More. When the screen says Hot, swirl in the oil. Wait a few seconds and put in the curry leaves. They will splatter, so stand back. Immediately add the ginger-garlic paste. Turn heat to Normal. Stir and sauté for 2–3 minutes, sprinkling a little water into the pot if seasonings start to stick. Add the chicken. Keep stirring for another 2 minutes, again sprinkling in a little water if anything seems to catch. Now add 1 cup water, the cilantro, and the garam masala. Stir to mix.

4. Hit CANCEL to reset the cooking program. Close and seal the lid and cook on LOW PRESSURE for 1 minute. Release the pressure manually. Take off the lid carefully, venting the remaining steam away from you. Select the SAUTÉ setting and set to More. Stir the yogurt mixture and pour it in. Bring to a simmer and cook for 5 minutes, stirring now and then, or until the sauce thickens. Turn the Instant Pot OFF or set to KEEP WARM as needed.

CHICKEN STEWED IN A LIGHT SAUCE WITH POTATOES AND CAULIFLOWER

SERVES 3-4

This dish is full of spice and flavor, yet it is very light. In our family, we tend to eat it over rice, but you could also serve it with some crusty bread.

Chicken thighs seem to be getting bigger by the day, so sometimes I ask my butcher to halve them crossways.

4 chicken thighs, halved, if possible (about 2 pounds)

Salt

Freshly ground pepper

1 tablespoon ground coriander

2 teaspoons ground cumin

½ teaspoon ground turmeric

½ teaspoon chili powder

½ teaspoon fenugreek seeds

1 teaspoon whole black peppercorns

2 teaspoons mustard powder

½ teaspoon fennel seeds

3 tablespoons peanut or olive oil

1 large onion, chopped

2 teaspoons peeled fresh ginger grated to a pulp

4 cups chicken stock or water

2 medium red potatoes (about 13 ounces in all), peeled and cut into 1-inch dice

8 medium cauliflower florets

1. Remove the chicken skins. Salt and pepper the thigh pieces lightly. You can do this a day before and then cover and refrigerate them. If you do not have the time, just do this when you start cooking.

2. Put the coriander, cumin, turmeric, chili powder, fenugreek seeds, black peppercorns, mustard powder, and fennel seeds into the container of a spice grinder or clean coffee grinder that is used only for spices. Grind until you have a fine powder.

3. Select the SAUTÉ setting on your Instant Pot and set to More for 30 minutes. When the screen says Hot, add oil, add the onions. Stir and sauté them for about 5 minutes or until they just start to turn brown. Add the ginger and stir a few times, then add the spices from the spice grinder and stir a few times. Put in the chicken pieces and stir a few times, then add the 4 cups stock or water and 1 teaspoon salt. Stir from the bottom, picking up all encrusted spices. Hit CANCEL to reset the cooking program.

4. Close and seal the lid. Cook at **LOW PRESSURE** for 6 minutes. Release the pressure manually and remove the lid.

5. Select the **SAUTÉ** setting and set to Normal for 30 minutes. When the sauce is bubbling, add the diced potatoes. Cook for 6–7 minutes or until the potatoes are almost done. Add the cauliflower, submerging the pieces in the sauce. Cook another 7–10 minutes or until the cauliflower is just done. Check the salt. You might want to add a bit more.

RED CHICKEN CURRY

SERVES 4–6

This delightful, spicy dish actually comes from India's neighbor, Sri Lanka. It gets its color from a freshly ground, bright red chili powder that is not always easy to find here. So I use a combination of chili powder and bright red paprika to achieve the same results. You may use a cut-up whole chicken here, as hosts in Sri Lanka did when I visited, or you may use the chicken parts that most please you, as I often do.

FOR THE MARINADE

3–3¼ pounds chicken thighs, or a whole chicken cut up into smaller serving pieces

2 tablespoons red wine vinegar

1¼ teaspoons salt, or to taste

¼–1 teaspoon chili powder

2½ tablespoons bright red paprika

½ teaspoon ground turmeric

1 tablespoon ground coriander

1½ teaspoons ground cumin

¼ teaspoon ground cinnamon

1½ teaspoons fennel seeds and ½ teaspoon fenugreek seeds, ground together in a clean coffee grinder (or buy both ground if you can get them)

2 tablespoons finely chopped shallots

FOR COOKING THE CHICKEN

4 tablespoons olive or peanut oil

1 cup finely sliced shallots

2 tablespoons peeled and coarsely chopped garlic

½ teaspoon whole fenugreek seeds

2 sticks of lemongrass, just the lower 6 inches, with the bulbous end lightly crushed

20 fresh curry leaves, if available

1 cup coconut milk from a well-shaken can

1. Remove as much skin and blobs of fat from the chicken as you can and put the chicken in a stainless steel or glass bowl. Add all the marinade ingredients and mix thoroughly. Cover and refrigerate overnight, or at least 6–8 hours.

2. Select the SAUTÉ setting on the Instant Pot and set to More. When the screen says Hot, swirl in the oil. Now put in the shallots and garlic. Stir and sauté for about 3 minutes, or until softened and golden. Add the fenugreek seeds and stir once or twice. Add the lemongrass and the curry leaves, slightly crushing the leaves in your palm as you put them into the pot. Add the marinated chicken and its juices. Stir for a minute, then add 1 cup water. Press CANCEL to reset the cooking program. Close and seal the lid. Set pressure release to Sealing. Cook at LOW PRESSURE for 6 minutes. Perform a quick release by turning the steam release handle on the lid to the Venting position. Hit CANCEL.

3. Open the pot carefully, venting the remaining steam away from you. Select the SAUTÉ setting and set to Less. Cover, either with the glass lid or loosely with the regular lid. Simmer gently for 7–10 minutes. Remove cover, add the coconut milk, mix, and taste for balance of flavors. Simmer for another 2 minutes.

ROYAL CHICKEN KORMA

SERVES 4–6

In India, dishes that contain expensive ingredients like saffron and nuts are associated with royalty and are generally reserved for special occasions.

Kormas, traditionally meat dishes, are cooked with yogurt, cream, or coconut milk to give them a creamy, rich taste. (For a vegetarian korma, see South Indian Mixed-Vegetable Korma, page 51.) In Britain, "korma" has come to mean a very mildly spiced dish, but this is not at all true in India. Indian kormas can be very spicy and hot.

A korma can be served with Indian flatbreads or an elegant rice dish, such as Basmati Rice Pilaf with Whole Garam Masala and Dill (page 121).

The whole spices are not meant to be eaten.

¼ cup heavy cream

A very generous pinch of saffron threads (more if you can afford it)

6 chicken thighs (about 3 pounds)

Salt

Freshly ground black pepper

4 tablespoons peanut or olive oil

3 tablespoons golden raisins

3 tablespoons slivered blanched almonds

5 whole green cardamom pods

1 medium stick cinnamon

1 medium onion, sliced into fine half-rings

1 tablespoon peeled fresh ginger grated to a pulp

4 cloves garlic, peeled and crushed to a pulp

1 tablespoon ground coriander

2 teaspoons ground cumin

½ cup plain yogurt

¼–1 teaspoon chili powder

½ teaspoon My Garam Masala (page 154)

1. Heat the cream in a microwave oven or in a small pot on the stove and then add the saffron. Set it aside for 2 hours to draw out the saffron color.

2. Skin the chicken thighs. Salt and pepper them lightly on both sides.

3. Select the **SAUTÉ** setting on your Instant Pot and set to More for 30 minutes. When the screen says Hot, swirl in the oil. Wait a few seconds and put in the golden raisins. Stir. They will swell up in a second. Remove them quickly with a slotted spoon and place in a bowl. Add the almonds to the oil. Stir. As soon as they turn golden, lift

them out with the slotted spoon and put in the bowl with the raisins. Put the cardamom pods and cinnamon stick in the pot and stir around for a few seconds. Put in the chicken, 2–3 pieces at a time, and brown them, about 3–4 minutes per side. As they get done, remove them to a bowl. Brown all the chicken this way. Now put the onions in the pot. Stir and fry them for 3–4 minutes or until they start to turn reddish. Add the ginger and garlic. Stir a few times, then add the coriander and cumin and stir once. Add a few tablespoons of water and scrape up what you can from the bottom of the pot. Return all the chicken pieces and their liquid to the pot. Add 1 tablespoon of yogurt at a time and stir it in until all the yogurt has been used up. Put in 1–1¼ teaspoons salt, chili powder, and ½ cup water. Hit **CANCEL** to reset the cooking program.

4. Close and seal the lid. Cook at **LOW PRESSURE** for 6 minutes and then release the pressure manually.

5. Remove the lid carefully, venting the remaining steam away from you. Select the **SAUTÉ** setting and set to Less. Cover with the glass lid or loosely with the regular lid. Simmer gently for 7–10 minutes. Add the garam masala and mix it in. Check for balance of flavors. Add the saffron cream and mix it in. Serve garnished with the raisins and almonds.

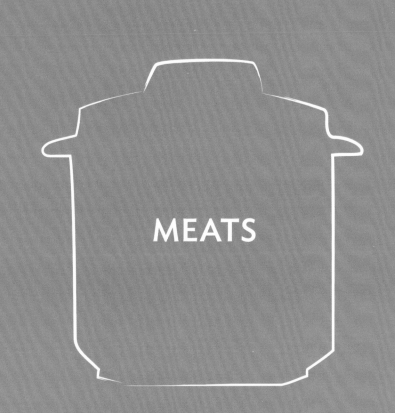

MEATS

GROUND LAMB WITH PEAS

Keema Matar

SERVES 3–4

Known as Keema Matar, this dish is loved by children, old people, and everyone in between. It is the first dish a young Indian abroad tries to cook, as it seems the most approachable. When I started writing cookbooks in America, I heard from so many college students who said that they learned to cook from my books and that the first dish they tried was this one. The seasonings I have used for this recipe are quite typical of the southern area in and around Hyderabad. Keema there was once considered a part of a leisurely Sunday breakfast offered to menfolk returning from a morning horse ride. The other dishes at breakfast would be khichri (dal and rice cooked together), crispy poppadums, and pickles.

In Delhi, where I was raised, this dish was served at lunch or dinner and usually with flatbreads like chapatis, parathas, and naans. (Pita-type breads would also do.) On the table would also be a vegetable dish, such as one made with cauliflower, a dal, a yogurt relish, and a small onion-tomato salad. You may also serve this with rice.

3 tablespoons peanut or olive oil

½ teaspoon whole black or brown mustard seeds

½ teaspoon whole cumin seeds

2 dried hot red chilies

10 fresh curry leaves, if available

½ cup finely chopped onions

2 cloves garlic, peeled and crushed to a pulp

2 teaspoons peeled fresh ginger grated to a pulp

1 pound ground lamb

1 tablespoon ground coriander

1 teaspoon ground cumin

4 tablespoons plain yogurt

1 cup peas, fresh or frozen and defrosted

¾ teaspoon salt

1. Select the SAUTÉ setting on your Instant Pot and set it to More. When the screen says Hot, swirl in the oil. Add the mustard seeds, cumin seeds, and red chilies. When the mustard seeds start to pop, turn the chilies over and put in the curry leaves. They will splutter, so stand back. Now quickly put in the onions. Stir and sauté for 4–5 minutes or until the onions start to brown. Add the garlic and ginger and stir a few times. Add the ground lamb and stir, breaking up all the lumps in the meat. Add the coriander and

cumin. Stir a few times, then add 1 tablespoon of the yogurt. Stir from the bottom as you continue to break up the lumps in the meat. Add the remaining yogurt, 1 tablespoon at a time the same way, as you continue to smash up the lumps and the yogurt gets absorbed. Add ¾ cup water and press CANCEL to reset the cooking program.

2. Close and seal the lid. Cook on HIGH PRESSURE for 10 minutes and then allow the pressure to drop by itself. Open the lid carefully, venting the remaining steam away from you. Select the SAUTÉ setting and set to Low. Add the peas and salt and stir to mix. Cook gently for 2–3 minutes if peas were frozen, 5–6 minutes if fresh, stirring now and then. Hit CANCEL when the peas are cooked through.

KERALA LAMB STEW

Eshtew

SERVES 4-6

Known locally as just *eshtew,* this classic dish with meat, potatoes, and vegetables is very popular with Kerala's Christian community, especially at Easter, when it is served with appams—steamed, spongy, savory rice cakes. Alas, there are no recipes for the appams in this book, but I generally serve this stew with plain rice anyway. You may also serve it with Plain Brown or Red Basmati Rice (page 118). This stew must have some British ancestry, but the spices it uses all grow in Kerala's backyards. It is generally cooked to be very spicy, so put in as many green chilies as you can easily manage.

Leave your can of coconut milk standing still, top up, for twenty-four hours. Just before using, open it carefully without tilting the can too much. Now, spoon off the very thick creamy coconut milk that has risen to the top and put it in a bowl. This is the thick coconut milk. The rest remaining in the can is the thin coconut milk.

4 tablespoons peanut or olive oil

3 whole green cardamom pods

1 medium stick cinnamon

3-4 whole cloves

About 30 fresh curry leaves, if available

1 large onion, cut into fine half-rings

2 teaspoons peeled fresh ginger grated to a pulp

2 pounds boneless lamb from the shoulder, cut into 1½-inch cubes

Salt

One 14-ounce can unsweetened coconut milk, separated into thin and thick coconut milk (see headnote)

3 large red potatoes, peeled and quartered

3 medium carrots, peeled and cut crosswise into 1-inch chunks

⅛–¼ teaspoon chili powder

1 teaspoon ground coriander

1-3 fresh hot bird's-eye chilies, with long slits cut lengthwise down their centers

1. Select the SAUTÉ setting on your Instant Pot and set to More, with the timer set for 30 minutes. When the screen says Hot, swirl in the oil. Then put in the cardamom, cinnamon, and cloves. Stir once or twice and put in half the curry leaves. They will splatter, so stand back. Quickly add the onions. Stir them until they are soft and just beginning to change color, about

5–6 minutes. Add the ginger and stir once or twice. Now put in all the meat and ¾ teaspoon salt. Stir the meat with the seasonings for 7–8 minutes, until it no longer appears red, then add ½ cup thin coconut milk and ½ cup water. Hit CANCEL to reset the cooking program. Close and seal the lid. Cook at HIGH PRESSURE for 20 minutes, then release the pressure manually.

2. While the meat cooks, put the potatoes and carrots in a bowl. Sprinkle ¼ teaspoon salt, the chili powder, and coriander over them and mix well. Throw the green chilies into the same bowl.

3. When all the pressure has been released from the Instant Pot, open the lid carefully, venting the remaining steam away from you. Add the carrots, potatoes, and chilies and stir to mix. Close and seal the lid once again and cook at LOW PRESSURE for 3 minutes. Release the pressure manually. Hit CANCEL. Remove the lid carefully, venting the remaining steam away from you. Select the SAUTÉ setting and set to Normal. Add ¾ cup thick coconut milk. Crush the remaining curry leaves in your hand and add them to the pot as well. Stir to mix and bring the stew to a simmer. Fish out the whole green chilies so they present no danger to the unsuspecting.

LAMB WITH SPINACH

Saag Gosht

SERVES 4–6

This dish is very popular throughout North India, eaten with Indian flatbreads or rice. I like it best when it is slow-cooked. I have just chopped the spinach finely here, but you could blanch it first in boiling water and chop finely or coarsely, as you wish.

5 tablespoons peanut or olive oil

2 pounds boneless lamb meat from the shoulder, cut into 1½–2-inch pieces and wiped dry

1 medium cinnamon stick

1¼ cups chopped onions

4 teaspoons of peeled fresh ginger grated to a pulp

4 cloves garlic, peeled and crushed

1 tablespoon ground coriander

2 teaspoons ground cumin

½ teaspoon ground turmeric

¼–1 teaspoon chili powder

⅓ cup peeled and chopped tomatoes (canned will do)

1 pound spinach, finely chopped (see headnote)

1¼ teaspoons salt

½ teaspoon My Garam Masala (page 154)

1. Select the SAUTÉ setting on your Instant Pot and set to More for 30 minutes. When the screen says Hot, swirl in the oil. Put in the dried-off pieces of lamb, a few at a time, and brown them. They will stick, but leave them alone until they unstick. Put them in a bowl as they brown. Do all the lamb this way. Then put the cinnamon into the pot. Stir once and add the onions. Stir and fry until the onions begin to turn brown, 6–7 minutes. Add the ginger and garlic and stir for a minute. Then add the coriander, cumin, turmeric, and chili powder. Stir once and put in the tomatoes. Stir, scraping up any crust stuck to the bottom. After a minute, pour in 1½ cups water and add the spinach and salt, stirring until the spinach wilts.

2. Add the meat. Close and lock the lid but *do not* seal it. Select the SLOW COOK setting and set the timer for 5 hours. When done, remove the lid carefully and check for salt. The sauce should be thick. If there is too much of it, boil some of it away by using the SAUTÉ setting set to Normal. Add the garam masala and stir it in.

RAJASTHANI RED BRAISED LAMB

Rajasthani Gosht

SERVES 4–6

In the deserts of Rajasthan, they like this dish very hot. It looks red when it appears on the table, from all the ground red chilies that go into the sauce. I make it less hot (you do not have to), but I try to get the same color by adding nice bright red paprika.

It is generally eaten with Indian flatbreads. You may buy some naan or whole-wheat pita breads to eat it with. Rice would be fine too. At a meal, I might include a green vegetable or the Sweet, Hot, and Sour Eggplants (page 39). Some kind of salad or a yogurt relish would round out a nice dinner.

¼ cup peanut or olive oil

2 medium cinnamon sticks

6 whole cloves

10 green cardamom pods

1 bay leaf

1 cup thinly sliced shallots

3 teaspoons finely grated peeled fresh ginger

4 cloves garlic peeled and crushed to a pulp

2 pounds boneless lamb from the shoulder, cut into 1½-inch cubes

1¼ teaspoons salt

¼–1 teaspoon chili powder

2 tablespoons bright red paprika

1 tablespoon ground coriander

1½ cups lamb stock or water

3 tablespoons chopped cilantro

Pour the oil into the inner container of the Instant Pot and select the SAUTÉ setting set to More. When the screen says Hot, put in the cinnamon sticks, cloves, cardamom, and bay leaf. Stir a few times, until the spices begin to darken. Quickly add the shallots. Stir and sauté for about 5 minutes or until the shallots just begin to brown. Add the ginger and garlic. Stir for another minute. Now add the lamb, salt, chili powder, paprika, and coriander. Stir a few times, then put in the stock or water. Close and seal the lid and cook on HIGH PRESSURE for 22 minutes, letting the pressure release naturally. Spoon out most of the fat. Serve garnished with cilantro.

BEEF OXTAIL IN A BAZAARI NORTH INDIAN RED SAUCE

Lal Gosht

SERVES 4

For those like me who like to eat around bones, this is a perfect dish.

Although Hindus generally do not eat beef, Indian Muslims and Christians do. This dish, along with braised shin meat and slow-cooked goat trotters, is often sold at street stalls in Muslim neighborhoods. Generally they are very spicy—and very red from chili powder—but you can control the heat by using less chili powder and fresh chilies. I use paprika to give the meat the red bazaar look. Normally served with soft Indian breads like naans, you may serve this with rice, rice noodles, or whole-wheat pita bread. A salad of sliced shallots (or onions), tomatoes, and cucumbers and a yogurt relish would make suitable accompaniments.

1½ teaspoons coriander seeds

1½ teaspoons cumin seeds

1 teaspoon fennel seeds

1 teaspoon black peppercorns

¼ teaspoon fenugreek seeds

One 4-inch piece peeled fresh ginger, chopped

4 cloves garlic, peeled and chopped

1–3 fresh hot green bird's-eye chilies, chopped

¼ teaspoon or more chili powder, as desired

½ teaspoon ground turmeric

2 teaspoons nice red paprika

4–5 tablespoons peanut or olive oil

2¾–3 pounds oxtail, cut into 1½-inch pieces and wiped dry with paper towels

1 medium cinnamon stick

5 whole green cardamom pods

1 cup thinly sliced shallots

1¼ teaspoons salt, or to taste

1. Put the coriander seeds, cumin seeds, fennel seeds, black peppercorns, and fenugreek seeds into a clean coffee grinder and grind until you have a fine powder.

2. Put the ginger, garlic, and green chilies into a blender along with ½ cup water. Blend until you have a smooth paste. Add the chili powder, turmeric, and paprika as well as the spices from the coffee grinder. Give the machine another whirr to mix all ingredients. This is the spice paste.

3. Pour 3 tablespoons of oil into the inner container of your Instant Pot and select the SAUTÉ setting, set to More. When the screen says

Hot, add enough of the meat pieces as will easily fit in a single layer. Brown on both sides and remove to a big bowl. Brown all the meat this way, adding more oil if needed.

4. When all the meat has been browned and removed to the bowl, add another tablespoon of oil to the Instant Pot. When the screen says Hot, put in the cinnamon stick and cardamom pods. Stir once or twice and add all the shallots to the pot. Stir and brown lightly, scraping up all the browned meat juices at the bottom. When the shallots are soft, add the paste from the blender. Stir and sauté for about 5 minutes.

5. Put all the meat and meat juices back into the pot, adding 1½ cups water and the salt. Stir to mix. Hit Cancel to reset the cooking program. Close and seal the lid, then select the **PRESSURE COOK** setting and set to high pressure, with the timer set for 55 minutes. When the time is up, let the pressure release naturally. Open carefully and remove as much of the fat as you can before serving.

GOAT CURRY

Bakri Ka Gosht

SERVES 4

This is the everyday goat curry served in much of North India and Pakistan. In our family we simply called it *gosht* or "meat." Most butchers in the West do not carry goat at all. But now, increasingly, there are many halal butchers in or near Indian, Pakistani, and Bangladeshi neighborhoods that do. You will also find it in West Indian neighborhoods.

In nearly all South Asian homes, the meat is cooked with the bone. It has much more flavor this way. Ask your butcher for some meat with bone from around the neck, some cut-up rib chops, some meat from the shank muscle (no bone here), and a few marrowbones with meat attached. Most of the pieces should be about 1½ inches in at least one direction. Wash the meat when you get it home and pat it dry.

Serve this with any flatbread or with rice.

2 pounds goat meat (see headnote)

5 tablespoons plain yogurt

4 tablespoons peanut or olive oil

1 medium onion, finely chopped

½–1 fresh hot green chili (like bird's-eye), chopped finely

One 3-inch piece peeled fresh ginger, grated to a pulp

4 cloves garlic, peeled and mashed to a pulp

2 teaspoons ground cumin

2 teaspoons ground coriander

¼–1 teaspoon chili powder

2 teaspoons bright red paprika

1 teaspoon salt

¾ cup peeled and chopped tomatoes (fresh or canned)

½ teaspoon My Garam Masala (page 154)

1. Combine the meat and yogurt in a bowl. Mix well and refrigerate overnight or for at least 3 hours.

2. Select the SAUTÉ setting on your Instant Pot, set to More, and set the timer for 30 minutes. When the screen says Hot, swirl in the oil. Put in all the meat and just let it sit there for a minute. Then stir it around for 7–8 minutes, until it is lightly browned in spots. Remove with a slotted spoon and save in a bowl. Put the onions and green chilies into the pot. Stir and cook for about 5–6 minutes or until the onions just start to

brown. Add the ginger and garlic and stir around a few times, then add the cumin, coriander, chili powder, paprika, and salt. Stir a few times, add the tomatoes, and stir and cook them until they thicken and you can see the oil at the edges of the spice paste. Add the meat and stir from the bottom for 2–3 minutes. Add ¾ cup water. Hit CANCEL to reset the cooking program.

3. Close and seal the lid. Cook at HIGH PRESSURE for 25 minutes, then let the pressure release naturally for 10 minutes, releasing the remaining pressure manually. Hit CANCEL. Take off the lid carefully, venting the remaining steam away from you. (You may also, as an alternative, cook the meat by selecting the SLOW COOKING setting set to Normal for 6 hours. Then proceed with what follows.)

4. Select the SAUTÉ setting set to Normal. Stir the meat and check the salt. When the sauce starts bubbling again, sprinkle the garam masala over the top and stir it in. Hit CANCEL or leave at KEEP WARM. Remove extra fat when serving.

INDIAN-CHINESE PORK CHOPS

SERVES 2–4

India has a tense, cold, mountainous, land border with China in the north, but all along the east, south, and west coasts of India, the two countries have traded by sea for at least a thousand years. Many Chinese people have settled in Chinatowns in port cities like Calcutta and Bombay, and a special Indochinese cuisine has developed in which soy sauce plays an integral part. This recipe, a creation of mine, is part of that tradition. It is also the first recipe that my children asked for when they left home to go to college. I have adapted it for the Instant Pot. It is important that the chops be thin and somewhat fatty.

Serve these chops with a rice dish.

4 center-cut pork chops, each about ½ inch thick (weighing about 1½ pounds in all)

3 tablespoons peanut or olive oil

1 medium stick cinnamon

6 whole cloves

1 teaspoon whole black peppercorns

1 bay leaf

1 medium onion, chopped

1 medium carrot, peeled and cut into ⅛-inch rounds

1 medium stick celery, halved lengthways and then cut crossways into ⅛-inch-wide pieces

3 tablespoons tamari soy sauce

1½ tablespoons sugar

¼ teaspoon chili powder

1. Pat the pork chops with a paper towel until they are quite dry.

2. Select the SAUTÉ setting on your Instant Pot and set to More for 30 minutes. When the screen says Hot, swirl in the oil. Put in two pork chops at a time to brown them. They will stick initially, but let them stay in place until they start to brown and loosen. Turn them over and brown the other side. When done, remove them to a bowl. Brown the remaining chops the same way and remove to the bowl. Then add the cinnamon, cloves, peppercorns, and bay leaf to the Instant Pot. Stir a few times. Now add the onions, carrots, and celery. Stir until all are lightly browned, 7–8 minutes. Hit CANCEL to reset the cooking program.

3. Now put the chops and their accumulated liquid back in the pan. Add ½ cup water, the tamari, sugar, and chili powder, and stir to mix.

4. The next step may be done one of two ways:

a. To pressure-cook: Close and seal the lid. Cook at **HIGH PRESSURE** for 20 minutes. Let the pressure drop naturally for 10 minutes and then release the remaining pressure manually. Hit **CANCEL** to reset the cooking program.

b. To slow-cook: Add another ½ cup water to the pot. Cover with the glass lid or use the regular lid, then lock but do not seal it. Select the **SLOW COOK** setting and set to Normal for 4 hours. When the time is up, hit **CANCEL** to reset the cooking program.

5. Remove the lid. Select the **SAUTÉ** setting and set to More to boil away most of the liquid, gently turning the chops in the sauce as you do so. You should end up with very little sauce left clinging to the chops.

PORK (OR LAMB) KABOBS

Bhunay Kabab

SERVES 4–6

In this recipe, which I created specifically for the pressure cooker more than two decades ago, I cook the pork cubes with just ginger, garlic, and a special mixture of spices (see Rai Masala on page 155). It is quite scrumptious, yet very easy to make in the Instant Pot. I buy cubed, boneless pork shoulder, cut into about 1–1½-inch cubes, and take off the larger hunks of fat from every piece. Just leave a sliver of fat, as that makes the meat very juicy. Those who do not eat pork may use lamb. (Although pork is more succulent.)

For a simple meal, just put these kabobs on top of rice, and add a further topping of slivered onions and tomatoes dressed with lime juice, salt, and chili powder. (See Onion-Tomato Salad, page 138.) You may also roll them in a soft flatbread with the same salad.

3 tablespoons peanut or olive oil

One 3-inch piece peeled fresh ginger, grated finely

4 cloves garlic, peeled and crushed to a pulp

2 pounds boneless pork shoulder, cut into 1–1½-inch cubes, heavy chunks of fat removed (see headnote)

2 tablespoons Rai Masala (page 155)

2 teaspoons ground cumin

½ teaspoon ground turmeric

¼–½ teaspoon chili powder

1 teaspoon salt

Freshly ground pepper

1½ tablespoons lemon juice, or to taste

1. Set the nonstick inner pot, if you have one, inside the Instant Pot (or use your stainless steel one). Select the SAUTÉ setting, set to More, and pour in the oil. When the screen says Hot, put in the ginger and garlic. Stir once or twice and add the pork cubes. Stir a few more times and put in the rai masala, cumin, turmeric, chili powder, salt, and pepper. Stir for about 2 minutes to mix all the spices, then add ½ cup water and mix it in.

2. Close and seal the lid and cook at HIGH PRESSURE for 20 minutes. Let the pressure drop naturally for 10 minutes, then release the remaining pressure manually. Remove the lid. Hit CANCEL to reset the cooking program, then select the SAUTÉ setting and set to MORE. Remove the meat with a slotted spoon and save it in a bowl. Meanwhile, boil down all the liquid

in the pot until you just have oil and a little of the spice mixture.

3. Add the meat back into the pot, still set to More, and stir it around, until lightly browned. Squeeze lemon juice over the top and mix it in.

4. Lift the meat out of the fat when serving but save the fat for storing leftovers, if there are any. The fat preserves the meat, almost like a confit.

GRAINS

PLAIN BASMATI RICE

Saaday Basmati Chawal

SERVES 4

Buy only the best basmati rice. It should be from India, as no other country grows anything comparable. The rice should look a bit yellow, because good basmati is always aged six months to a year before it is sold. Ask your Indian grocer for help. Even I do that, as the quality of different varieties goes up and down.

2 cups basmati rice

1. Put the rice in a bowl. Add cold water from the faucet to cover generously and swish the rice around with your hand. Pour out most of the water. Do this 4–5 times, until the water seems reasonably clear. Pour in enough water to cover the rice by 2 inches and set aside for 30 minutes. Empty the rice into a fine strainer. Set the strainer over the now-empty bowl and put aside as you set up your Instant Pot.

2. Put the rice and 2⅔ cup water into the Instant Pot, ensuring that no rice lands on the lip of the inner pot. Make sure that the rice is more or less level, then close and lock the lid, setting the PRESSURE RELEASE to Sealing. Select the RICE setting. When the program finishes, leave the Instant Pot on the KEEP WARM setting for 10 minutes. Then turn the PRESSURE RELEASE to Venting to release the remaining steam. Open the pot carefully, venting the remaining steam away from you. Use the rice paddle to remove the rice.

PLAIN JASMINE RICE

SERVES 4

India does not grow jasmine rice, but we do have many other rices that are similar.

2 cups jasmine rice

1. Put the rice in a bowl. Add cold water from the faucet to cover generously and swish the rice around with your hand. Pour out most of the water. Do this 4–5 times, until the water seems reasonably clear. Empty the rice into a fine strainer. Set the strainer over the now-empty bowl and set aside as you set up your Instant Pot.

2. Put the rice and 2⅔ cups water into the Instant Pot, making sure that no rice lands on the lip of the inner pot. The rice should be more or less level. Close and lock the lid, setting PRESSURE RELEASE to Sealing. Select the RICE setting. When the program finishes, leave the Instant Pot on the KEEP WARM setting for 10 minutes. Then turn the PRESSURE RELEASE to Venting to release the remaining steam. Open the pot carefully, venting the remaining steam away from you. Use the rice paddle to remove the rice.

PLAIN BROWN OR RED BASMATI RICE

SERVES 4

In America, we have always been able to find a lot of brown basmati rice (Indian is best), but are now also beginning to see red basmati rice from Sri Lanka. (Kalustyan's in New York carries it.) The hull of this grain is a lovely dark red color. It is nutty, very delicious, and cooks beautifully in the Instant Pot. Indians tend not to use salt when they cook plain rice, as everything it is eaten with is generally so highly seasoned, but if you wish, you may add up to a teaspoon of salt. You may also cook this rice with chicken stock instead of water.

In this recipe, I let the rice soak in the Instant Pot itself.

1 cup brown or red basmati rice

1⅓ cups chicken stock or water

1 teaspoon salt, if desired

1. Put the rice in a bowl. Add cold water from the faucet to cover generously and swish the rice around with your hand. Pour out most of the water. Do this 4–5 times, until the water seems reasonably clear. Empty the rice into a fine strainer. Set the strainer over the now-empty bowl and put aside as you set up your Instant Pot.

2. Put the rice and the 1⅓ cups water or stock into the Instant Pot, making sure that no rice lands on the lip of the inner pot. The rice should be more or less level. Leave to soak for 30 minutes. Close and lock the lid, setting the **PRESSURE RELEASE** to Sealing. Cook on **HIGH PRESSURE** for 20 minutes. Let the pressure release naturally for 10 minutes, and then turn the **PRESSURE RELEASE** to Venting to release the remaining steam. Open the pot carefully, venting the remaining steam away from you. Use the rice paddle to remove the rice.

BASMATI RICE PILAF WITH PEAS

Tahiri

SERVES 4

Fresh peas were available only in the winter when I was growing up in India, so that is when we ate this dish. In America, we can get very good-quality frozen peas all year round, so it is never a problem to make this tahiri. Here is how to treat the peas:

For fresh peas that are young and sweet: Drop them into salted boiling water for 1–2 minutes, just enough to cook them. Drain them and then refresh them under cold water.

For frozen peas: Drop them into salted boiling water for 10 seconds, then drain and refresh under cold water.

2 cups basmati rice

2 tablespoons peanut or olive oil

½ teaspoon whole cumin seeds

1 bay leaf

1 cup fine half-moon slices from a small onion or a large shallot

2⅔ cups chicken stock (or vegetable stock if you are vegetarian)

1 teaspoon salt (use 1½ teaspoons salt if the stock is unsalted)

1 cup peas, fresh or frozen (see headnote)

1. Put the rice in a bowl. Add cold water from the faucet to cover generously and swish the rice around with your hand. Pour out most of the water. Do this 4–5 times, until the water seems reasonably clear. Pour in enough water to cover the rice by 2 inches. Leave to soak for 30 minutes. Strain. Set the strainer over the now-empty bowl and set aside as you get your Instant Pot ready.

2. Select the SAUTÉ setting on your Instant Pot and set to More. When the screen says Hot, swirl in the oil. Wait a few seconds, then add the cumin seeds and bay leaf. Stir once or twice as the spices darken. Now add the onions and stir for about 5 minutes or until the onions begin to turn brown. Add the drained rice, making sure that no rice lands on the lip of the inner pot. Stir very gently from the bottom with a flat spatula for a minute, making sure not to break the grains of rice. Add the stock and salt. Make sure that the rice is more or less level, then hit CANCEL to reset the cooking program.

3. Close and seal the lid. Select the RICE setting. When the program finishes, leave the Instant Pot on the KEEP WARM setting for 10 minutes, then turn the pressure release to Venting to release the remaining steam. Open the pot carefully, venting the remaining steam away from you. Quickly scatter the peas over the rice and close the lid but do not seal it. Let the peas heat up for 10 minutes. When serving, mix the rice and peas gently, using the paddle. Use the rice paddle to remove the rice. The best way to do this is to lift up a lump, then press down on it with the paddle gently to separate the rice grains.

BASMATI RICE PILAF WITH WHOLE GARAM MASALA AND DILL

Sooay Kay Chawal

SERVES 4

The way I see it, the Instant Pot has mastered rice cooking. Any of you who are afraid of making a complicated basmati rice pilaf need worry no more. The machine will practically make it for you. Just get a good-quality Indian basmati. Even I do not always know which it is, so I ask an Indian grocer, "What is your best Indian basmati?" Often it is a bit yellower, as it has been aged.

I love this pilaf and make it often when I am entertaining. The large spices are not meant to be eaten. You may remove them or leave them as a garnish, the way Indians do.

2 cups basmati rice

2 tablespoons peanut or olive oil

1 medium cinnamon stick

5 green cardamom pods

1 bay leaf

1 cup fine half-moon slices cut from an onion or a large shallot

¾ packed cup finely chopped dill feathers (not the coarse stems)

2⅔ cups chicken stock (or vegetable stock if you are vegetarian)

1 teaspoon salt (use 1½ teaspoons salt if the stock is unsalted)

1. Put the rice in a bowl. Add cold water from the faucet to cover generously and swish the rice around with your hand. Pour out most of the water. Do this 4–5 times, until the water seems reasonably clear. Pour in enough water to cover the rice by 2 inches and set aside for 30 minutes. Empty the rice into a fine strainer. Set the strainer over the now-empty bowl and set aside as you get your Instant Pot ready.

2. Select the **SAUTÉ** setting on your Instant Pot and set to More. When the screen says Hot, swirl in the oil. Wait a few seconds and then add the cinnamon stick, cardamom pods, and bay leaf. Stir once or twice as the spices darken. Now add the onions and stir for about 5 minutes or until the onions begin to turn brown. Add the drained rice and the dill, making sure that no rice lands on the lip of the inner pot. Stir very gently from the bottom with a flat spatula for a minute, making sure not to break the grains of rice. Add

the stock and salt. Make sure that the rice is more or less level, then hit CANCEL to reset the cooking program.

3. Close and seal the lid. Select the RICE setting. When the program finishes, leave the Instant Pot on the KEEP WARM setting for 10 minutes. Then turn the pressure release to Venting to release the remaining steam. Open the pot carefully, venting the remaining steam away from you. Use the rice paddle to remove the rice. The best way to do this is to first remove a lump of rice, then press gently on it with the paddle to separate the grains.

SAFFRON RICE WITH GOLDEN RAISINS

Zaafraan Uar Kishmish Ka Pullao

SERVES 6

This slightly sweet and slightly salty pilaf is best served at special occasions. I once used at least two teaspoons of saffron threads for this recipe, but it has become so expensive that even I have cut down now and cheat by adding a pinch of egg coloring to my saffron milk. This way I get both the full color and that lovely true saffron aroma. If you wish to cheat a bit too, look for egg coloring in Indian stores. Get the saffron color.

When this dish is done, you will have a mixture of white and saffron-colored rice grains, a very nice effect. Of course, you must use the best Indian basmati rice here.

1 tablespoon hot milk

2 teaspoons sugar

Two generous pinches of good-quality saffron threads

2 cups basmati rice

3 tablespoons peanut oil or ghee

3 tablespoons golden raisins

1 medium stick cinnamon

5 whole green cardamom pods

1 bay leaf

1 teaspoon salt

1. Mix the hot milk and sugar together in a very small bowl. Add the saffron, mix, and set aside for 2–3 hours.

2. Put the rice in a bowl. Add cold water from the faucet to cover generously and swish the rice around with your hand. Pour out most of the water. Do this 4–5 times, until the water seems reasonably clear. Pour in enough water to cover the rice by 2 inches and set aside for 30 minutes. Strain. Set the strainer over the now-empty bowl and set aside as you get your Instant Pot ready.

3. Select the SAUTÉ setting on your Instant Pot and set to More. When the screen says Hot, add the oil or ghee, then put in the golden raisins. Stir until they all plump up. Remove them quickly and save in a bowl. Add the cinnamon stick, cardamom pods, and bay leaf to the Instant Pot and stir a few times. Now put in all the drained rice and stir it very gently from the bottom for a minute. Add 2⅔ cups water and salt. Hit CANCEL to reset the cooking program.

4. Close and seal the lid and select the RICE setting. When the program finishes, leave the Instant Pot on the KEEP WARM setting for 10 minutes. Then turn the pressure release to Venting to release the remaining steam. Open the pot carefully, venting the remaining steam away from you. Quickly dribble the saffron mixture over parts of the rice. Put the raisins on top. Close the lid again, but do not seal it. Leave on KEEP WARM for at least 10 minutes. Use the rice paddle to remove the rice. The best way to do this is to remove just a lump first, then press down on it with the paddle gently to separate the rice grains.

LAMB PILAF

Yakhni Pullao

SERVES 4–5

In our North Indian home, we were often served this pilaf for Sunday lunch. It is considered quite special—elegant, highly aromatic, but not at all spicy. First a soup—or *yakhni*—is made with lamb, well flavored with fennel, ginger, onions, and cloves. The rice is then cooked in this soup, instead of in plain water: hence its Indian name, Yakhni Pullao. As the meat is added, the dish becomes even more alluring. You should use the very best-quality Indian basmati rice here. Because it is aged, it will be yellowish in color.

Serve with a yogurt relish, such as yogurt with Cucumbers, Tomatoes, and Onions (page 147), a vegetable dish such as Sweet, Hot, and Sour Eggplants (page 39), and perhaps a store-bought pickle.

I use the slow-cooking technique to make the soup. Since it takes five hours, either plan on starting early or make the soup the day before and leave the next day for cooking the rice. A night in the refrigerator will help you take the fat off the soup with much greater ease.

FOR THE SOUP

½ medium onion

One 1-inch piece of peeled fresh ginger

3 cloves garlic

7 whole cloves

About 20 whole peppercorns

1 medium stick cinnamon

3 bay leaves

1 teaspoon whole cumin seeds

2 teaspoons whole fennel seeds

2 teaspoons whole coriander seeds

3 large black cardamom pods (or 4 green cardamom pods)

4 cups chicken or lamb stock (beef stock will also do)

¾ teaspoon salt

1¼ pounds lamb meat from the shoulder, cut into 1½–2-inch pieces

YOU WILL ALSO NEED

2 cups basmati rice (see headnote)

4 tablespoons peanut or olive oil

½ medium onion, cut into very fine half-rings

1 teaspoon whole cumin seeds

2 large black cardamom pods (or 4 green cardamom pods)

2 tablespoons plain yogurt

1. Spread a 10-inch square of tripled-up cheesecloth on the counter. In the center, place the ½ medium onion, the piece of ginger, the garlic, cloves, peppercorns, cinnamon stick, bay leaves, 1 teaspoon cumin seeds, fennel seeds, coriander seeds, and 3 black cardamom pods. Tie up this bundle and put it in the inner container of the Instant Pot. Add the stock, salt, and lamb. Put on the glass cover or use the regular lid but *do not seal* it. Select the SLOW COOK setting and set it to Normal for 5 hours.

2. When the time is up, remove the lid. Wearing oven mitts, lift out the inner pot. Wring out and then throw away the bundle of seasonings. Remove all the meat with a slotted spoon and place in a bowl to cool. Strain the stock through a fine sieve and leave in another bowl to cool. If you have the time, cover and refrigerate the soup and the meat separately, and remove the fat when you take the soup back out. If you do not have time, scoop out as much fat from the soup as you can and set the meat and the soup aside, separately. Wash and dry the inner pot and put it back in its housing.

3. Put the rice in a bowl. Add cold water from the faucet to cover generously and swish the rice around with your hand. Pour out most of the water. Do this 4–5 times, until the water seems reasonably clear. Pour in enough water to cover the rice by 2 inches and set aside for half an

hour. Empty the rice into a wire mesh strainer. Set the strainer over the now-empty bowl and set aside.

4. Line a plate with paper towels and keep it near you. Make sure that the meat and stock are nearby as well.

5. Select the SAUTÉ setting on your Instant Pot and set to Normal for 30 minutes. When the screen says Hot, swirl in the oil. Put in the onions. Stir and fry the half-rings. As some of them begin to darken, change the SAUTÉ setting to Less. Keep frying and stirring until all the onion slivers are reddish brown and crisp. Lift them out with a slotted spoon and spread them on the paper towel. They will turn even more crisp as they sit.

6. Put the remaining 1 teaspoon cumin seeds and the cardamom pods into the oil in the pot. Stir for a few seconds. Now add all the meat. Stir it with a gentle hand until it starts to brown. Add 1 tablespoon of yogurt and keep stirring gently until it is absorbed. Add the second tablespoon of yogurt and let it get absorbed as well. Remove all the meat and keep it in a bowl. Quickly add 2⅔ cup of the newly made stock to the pot and scrape up the bottom. Add the rice, making sure that it is evenly spread out. Now close and seal the lid and select the RICE setting. When the program finishes, leave the Instant Pot on the KEEP WARM setting for 10 minutes. Then turn the pressure release to Venting to release the

remaining steam. Open the pot carefully, venting the remaining steam away from you. Remove the lid and quickly spread all the meat over the rice. Put the lid back on. Lock it, but *do not seal*. Select the KEEP WARM setting for at least another 10 minutes to warm up the meat. When serving, mix the rice and meat together gently, breaking up lumps by pressing down on them with a paddle, and strew the fried onions over the top.

QUINOA WITH TOMATOES

Quinoa Upma

SERVES 4

In India, an *upma* is traditionally a spicy rice-like dish made with semolina. It is originally from southern and western India, but today it is made all over the country with all manner of grains. I have even seen it made with bread! As new grains enter the country, Indians make upmas with it. Quinoa is just one of the latest.

Quinoa contains bitter saponins that need to be washed off. This is not easy, since the grains are so small. I prefer to buy quinoa that is already washed. Look at the label carefully when you buy it, and make sure it says "Washed."

Upmas may be served in a bowl and eaten as is or with yogurt relishes, pickles, and chutneys. A salad may be served on the side. Indians tend to eat them as a quick meal or snack.

2 tablespoons peanut or olive oil

¼ teaspoon whole black mustard seeds

¼ teaspoon whole cumin seeds

1 dried hot red chili

8–10 fresh curry leaves, if available

⅓ cup finely chopped shallots

2 tablespoons finely chopped fresh mint leaves

2 tablespoons finely chopped fresh cilantro

1–2 fresh hot green chilies (like bird's-eye), chopped

1 cup peeled and finely chopped tomatoes

1 cup quinoa

1¼ teaspoons salt

1. Select the **SAUTÉ** setting on your Instant Pot and set to More for 30 minutes. When the screen says Hot, add oil, put in the mustard seeds, cumin seeds, and red chili. Stir a few times until the chili turns dark on both sides. Add the curry leaves. They will splatter, so stand back. Quickly put in the shallots and stir for a few minutes or until they just start to brown. Add the mint, cilantro, and green chilies. Stir a few times. Add the tomatoes. Stir until the tomatoes break down a bit. Add the quinoa and stir gently a few times. Now add 1½ cups water and salt. Hit **CANCEL** to reset the cooking program.

2. Close and seal the lid and select the **RICE** setting. When the program finishes, leave on the **KEEP WARM** setting for 10 minutes. Then turn the pressure release to Venting to release the remaining steam. Open the pot carefully, venting the remaining steam away from you. Immediately cover the pot with a tea towel to absorb some of the moisture.

SIDE DISHES

AVOCADO-RADISH SALAD

SERVES 1

North Indians make this kind of quick salad all the time, using whatever ingredients they have. Most of the time in the summer it is tomatoes and onions and cucumbers, but in the winters it could include radishes and young kohlrabis. I was just sitting working one day and I needed a quick lunch. So I heated up some Black-eyed Peas with Mushrooms (page 27), which I had made the night before, and then I looked around. There was an avocado in the refrigerator and some radishes in the garden. I made a quick salad of the two and had my meal with whole-grain bread. It was wonderful. You do not need too many ingredients for this salad. And I won't even provide you with the exact measurements—you can just taste and go. Make the salad at the last moment, or it will get watery.

¼–½ avocado, peeled and
    diced
3–4 radishes, cut crossways
    into thick slices
Lemon juice
Salt
Freshly ground pepper
Ground roasted cumin seeds
    (page 152), optional
Chili powder

Put the avocado and radishes into a bowl. Squeeze lemon juice over them. Now add generous pinches of salt, pepper, cumin, and chili power. Toss to mix.

BABY ARUGULA SALAD WITH MUSTARD OIL

SERVES 4

Here is my slightly Indianized dressing flavored with mustard oil that I often use for salads served with Indian food. You can make the salad with baby arugula or a selection of microgreens like mâche. Always dress the leaves very lightly, reserving any remaining dressing for future use. There is enough dressing here for 5–6 cups of greens.

2 tablespoons olive oil

2 teaspoons mustard oil

2 teaspoons lemon juice

¼ teaspoon salt

Freshly ground black pepper

Put all the ingredients in a small jar. Shake until well mixed. Dress salads with a very light hand. Save remaining dressing for the future.

CUCUMBER, ONION, AND TOMATO SALAD

SERVES 4

There are so many variations of this everyday salad, eaten by Indians of all classes. Almost the same ingredients can easily be converted into a raita by adding yogurt (page 147).

1 cup peeled seedless
    cucumber cut into ½-inch
    dice
1 cup peeled tomatoes cut
    into ½-inch dice
1 cup onion cut into ½-inch
    dice
½ teaspoon salt
Freshly ground black pepper
½ teaspoon ground roasted
    cumin seeds (page 152)
⅛–½ teaspoon chili powder
1 tablespoon lime or lemon
    juice

Put the cucumbers, tomatoes, and onions in a bowl. Shortly before eating, add the salt, pepper, cumin, chili powder, and the lime or lemon juice. Mix and taste for balance of flavors.

ONION-TOMATO SALAD

SERVES 4

This is a very common, simple salad. It is best made just shortly before eating. You may add cilantro or mint to it as well.

1 cup fine onion or shallot slivers

½ cup firm, medium-sized tomatoes cut into fine wedges

1 tablespoon lemon juice

¼ teaspoon salt, or to taste

¼ teaspoon ground roasted cumin seeds (page 152)

A dusting of chili powder

Mix all ingredients together in a bowl.

CILANTRO CHUTNEY

SERVES 6–8

1 well-packed cup cilantro
  leaves
2–3 fresh hot green chilies,
  chopped
½ teaspoon salt
1 tablespoon lemon juice
1 cup plain yogurt

1. Put the cilantro, chilies, salt, lemon juice, and 3 tablespoons water into a blender. Blend, pushing down with a rubber spatula as needed, until smooth.

2. Put the yogurt in a bowl. Beat lightly with a whisk or fork until smooth and creamy. Add the contents of the blender and mix it in. Taste for balance of seasonings.

FRESH TOMATO CHUTNEY

SERVES 6

Not unlike a salsa, this is a simple fresh chutney to have on the table.

2 cups peeled and finely
    chopped fresh tomatoes
1 cup fresh cilantro leaves,
    chopped
1–4 fresh hot green chilies,
    chopped
½–¾ teaspoon salt

Combine the tomatoes, cilantro, and chilies in a bowl. Mix. Add the salt just before serving and mix it in.

EASY TAMARIND CHUTNEY

MAKES A GENEROUS ½ CUP

This hot, sweet, and sour chutney is really a revelation of the Indian palate in a bowl. This is what gets our juices flowing. It is intense—but then, we never use too much of it. It is an accent that we add to many foods: You can dribble it over yogurt or banana slices as a relish, or you can use it as a dip with French fries (see Spicy Fat French Fries, page 49), among other things. It will last several weeks in the refrigerator and can also be frozen.

This recipe requires tamarind paste. You can make your own, if you wish. Follow the instructions on p. 155. This is what I generally do. But when I'm in a rush, I follow an easier method.

All Indian grocers now sell bottled tamarind pastes. Even some general specialty food shops carry them. (Just do not get tamarind concentrate, which is a different thing.) Most tamarind pastes vary a bit, so you may need to alter the amounts of water, sugar, and salt you add. You are aiming for a thick but flowing sauce.

Very finely chopped fresh mint or finely crumbled dried mint is sometimes added to this chutney.

4 tablespoons tamarind paste

5 tablespoons sugar

½ teaspoon salt, or to taste

1 teaspoon ground roasted cumin seeds (page 152)

A general sprinkling of chili powder

Combine all the ingredients along with 2 tablespoons water. Mix thoroughly, tasting for balance of flavors.

YOGURT WITH CARROTS AND RAISINS

Gajar Aur Kishmish Ka Raita

SERVES 4–6

A sweet and sour relish that is perfect with most Indian meals.

4 tablespoons golden raisins

1½ cups plain yogurt

½ teaspoon salt

1 tablespoon sugar

2 medium carrots, peeled and
　coarsely grated

1 tablespoon peanut or olive
　oil

¼ teaspoon whole black
　mustard seeds

1. Soak the raisins in boiling water to cover generously for 3 hours. Drain.

2. Put the yogurt into a bowl. Beat lightly with a fork or whisk until smooth. Add the salt, sugar, and carrots. Mix well.

3. Put the oil in a small pot or small frying pan and set at medium-high heat. When very hot, add the mustard seeds. They will begin to pop in seconds. Pour the oil and spices over the yogurt and mix them in. Keep covered and refrigerated until needed.

YOGURT AND APPLE RAITA

SERVES 4–6

1¼ cups plain yogurt

About ¼ teaspoon salt

Freshly ground black pepper

⅛ teaspoon chili powder

½ peeled apple, cut into small
   dice

Put the yogurt in a bowl. Beat lightly with a fork or whisk until smooth and creamy. Add all the remaining ingredients and mix well.

YOGURT WITH CUCUMBER AND MINT

Kheeray Ka Raita

SERVES 6

This simple raita may be served with almost any Indian meal.

2 cups plain yogurt

¾ teaspoon salt

⅛ teaspoon chili powder

½ teaspoon ground roasted
cumin seeds (page 152)

1 medium cucumber, peeled
and grated

2 tablespoons very finely
chopped fresh mint

Put the yogurt in a bowl. Whisk it lightly with a fork or small whisk until smooth. Add all the other ingredients and mix. Taste for balance of flavors. Cover and refrigerate until needed.

YOGURT WITH CUCUMBERS, TOMATOES, AND ONIONS

Salaad Ka Raita

SERVES 4

An everyday raita, but one that goes particularly well with pilafs. You can add chopped-up hot green chilies, as well.

1 cup plain yogurt

½ teaspoon salt

Freshly ground black pepper

⅛–¼ teaspoon chili powder

½ teaspoon ground roasted cumin seeds (page 152)

½ cup peeled seedless cucumber cut into ⅓-inch dice

½ cup peeled fresh tomato cut into ⅓-inch dice

⅓ cup onions cut into ⅓-inch dice

Put the yogurt in a bowl. Beat lightly with a whisk or fork until smooth and creamy. Add the salt, pepper, chili powder, and cumin. Stir to mix. Add the cucumbers, tomatoes, and onions. Mix gently.

CROUTONS

SERVES 4–6

I do not know why it is, but Indians love croutons with their soups. The British gave us soups when they ruled us, and we Indianized them. However, the croutons we seem to have accepted just the way they were and left them untouched. They were always fried in our home, but here I have baked them in an oven. I used Pepperidge Farm bread, but you can use any bread you prefer.

4 slices Pepperidge Farm
   sliced bread

2 tablespoons peanut or olive
   oil or softened butter

1. Preheat oven to 350°F.

2. Brush the slices of bread on both sides with the oil or butter. Stack the slices on top of each other and cut the crusts off. Now cut the slices into croutons about ⅓–½-inch wide, or larger if you prefer. Spread out on a baking tray and bake for 7–8 minutes. Turn the croutons over and bake another 7–8 minutes. Allow to cool, and store in a ziplock bag.

RICE NOODLES

Sevai, Idiappam

SERVES 4

South India specializes in the most wonderful thin rice noodles. Known as *sevai* or *idiappam,* they are made at home from a ground rice dough that is extruded from a special gadget onto an oiled plate and then steamed. They may be eaten with cardamom-flavored coconut milk for breakfast but are mostly served with spicy curries. Some Indians do make these noodles in their American homes, but most just use dried rice noodles such as thin rice sticks and the wider, Vietnamese-named *banh pho* found in Southeast Asian markets. Here is a recipe for cooking *banh pho.* They are stiff, translucent, flat, and about ¼ inch wide and often sold in 1-pound packets. Half the packet will serve 4 people.

8 ounces rice noodles (*banh pho*)

1 teaspoon peanut or olive oil, or more as needed

1. Put the noodles in a large bowl. Cover well with water and leave to soak for 2 hours. Drain.

2. Bring a large pot of water to a rolling boil as you would for pasta. Once it is boiling, drop in the noodles. Cook for 1 minute or less, until just done. The water may or may not come to a boil again. Drain and rinse the noodles in cold running water to wash away the starch. Drain again and put in a bowl. Pour 1 teaspoon oil over the noodles and toss. The noodles are now ready to be stir-fried, put into soups, or reheated. To reheat, drop into boiling water for a second. Then drain and rub again with a little oil or they will be sticky.

Spices and Special Ingredients

ASAFETIDA

The sap from the roots and stem of a giant fennel-like plant dries into a hard resin. It is sold in both lump and ground form. Only the ground form is used in this book. It has a strong fetid aroma and is used in very small quantities both for its legendary digestive properties and for the much gentler, garlic-like aroma it leaves behind after cooking. (James Beard compared it to the smell of truffles.) It is excellent with dried beans and vegetables. Store in a tightly closed container. Flour is usually added in the processing, but it is now available in a gluten-free form from Kalustyan's in New York City.

CHICKPEA FLOUR

A very fine and nutritionally rich flour made out of ground chickpeas. It is sold in all specialty stores and by Indian grocers, where it is sometimes labeled gram flour or besan.

CHILIES, FRESH GREEN AND RED

The fresh green chili used in Indian cooking is of the cayenne type, generally about 1½–3 inches long and slender. Its heat can vary from mild to fiery. I like to use bird's-eye chilies, as they are most like Indian chilies. The only way to judge the heat is by breaking a chili in half and tasting a tiny piece of skin from the middle section. (Keep some yogurt handy!) The top part of the chili with more seeds is always the hottest, the bottom tip, the mildest. The hot seeds of the chili are never removed in India, but you may do so if you wish. Use whatever chili you can find. Chilies are a very rich source of iron and vitamins A and C. To store fresh red or green chilies, wrap them first in newspaper, then in plastic, and store in the refrigerator. They should last several weeks. Any that begin to soften and rot should be removed, as they tend to infect the whole batch. Fresh chilies may also be frozen. That is how I keep mine, removing a few from the freezer as I need them.

CHILIES, DRIED HOT RED

Buy these chilies from Indian grocers. They are usually quite hot and about 1½ inches long.

CUMIN SEEDS, GROUND ROASTED
MAKES ABOUT 3½ TABLESPOONS

Roasting brings out a darker, stronger aroma from cumin seeds. This taste and aroma is required for some cooked dishes and for many salads, relishes, and snack foods.

3 tablespoons whole cumin seeds

Put a small cast-iron or other heavy frying pan on medium-high heat. When hot, scatter in the cumin seeds. Stir and roast until the seeds are a shade darker and emit a roasted aroma. This happens in minutes. Empty the seeds onto a sheet of paper towel. Spread them out and let them cool, then put them into a clean coffee grinder or other spice grinder and grind as finely as possible. Store in a jar with a tight lid, away from dampness and light. This will last several months.

CURRY LEAVES, FRESH

These highly aromatic leaves are used in much coastal and southern Indian cookery. They are always used in their fresh form. They are now increasingly available in the West. Indian grocers sell both fresh and dried curry leaves, but buy only the fresh ones, which come still attached to their stalks. The leaves can be pulled off the stalks in one swoop. Keep curry leaves in a flat plastic bag. They last for several days in the refrigerator. If fresh curry leaves are not obtainable, omit them from the recipe.

CHILI POWDER

Chili powder just means powdered dried red chilies. Sometimes Indians use lots of chili powder to make a dish both hot and red. To get the color without all of the heat, add fresh bright red paprika. (Very old paprika tends to darken.)

DAL

In India the general word for beans and split peas is *dal*. The older they are, the longer they take to cook. If not soft in the time suggested, give another 5–10 minutes, still under pressure.

Store in tightly closed jars. All beans should be picked over and washed in several changes of water before cooking.

GHEE (CLARIFIED BUTTER)

This is butter that has been so thoroughly clarified that it can even be used for deep-frying. As it no longer contains milk solids, refrigeration is not necessary. It has a nutty, buttery taste. All Indian grocers sell it, and I find it more convenient to buy it than to make it from scratch.

GINGER, FRESH

This rhizome has a sharp, pungent, cleansing taste and is a digestive to boot. It is ground and used in meat sauces and in drinks. It is also cut into slivers or minute dice and used when stir-frying potatoes, green beans, spinach, and other vegetables. When finely grated ginger is required, it should first be peeled and then grated on the finest part of a grater so it turns into pulp. When a recipe requires that 1 inch of ginger be grated, it is best to keep that piece attached to the large knob. The knob acts as a handle and saves you from grating your fingers.

MY GARAM MASALA
MAKES ABOUT 3 TABLESPOONS

Almost every family in India has its own garam masala recipe, all differing slightly from each other. *Garam* means "hot" and *masala* means "spices." But the "hot" in *garam* refers to spices that heat the body, not spiciness. Garam masalas not only heat the body, they are also very aromatic. They can be used whole or ground and tend to include cloves, cinnamon, nutmeg, black peppercorns, black cumin, and black cardamom. Many people substitute green cardamom for the black (I do) and regular cumin for the black (I don't).

All these spices are relatively expensive. In commercially prepared garam masalas, many cheaper fillers, like coriander, are thrown in, so the aroma and intensity of the mix is lessened. When I say "My Garam Masala" in a recipe, I am referring to my more concentrated, highly aromatic mix.

Most Indian grocers sell cardamom seeds, so you do not have to sit around peeling cardamom pods!

1 tablespoon cardamom seeds
1 teaspoon black peppercorns
1 teaspoon black cumin (also called *shah zeera*)
1 teaspoon whole cloves
One 2-inch stick of cinnamon, broken up
⅓ whole nutmeg seed (just hit the seed with a hammer)

Put all the spices into the container of a clean coffee grinder or spice grinder and grind as finely as possible. Store the mixture in a jar with a tight lid, away from dampness and light. It should last several months.

Kalustyan's, in New York City, is now selling My Garam Masala as Madhur Jaffrey's Garam Masala, using this very recipe. You may buy it from them if you wish.

OIL

My preference is for peanut oil or olive oil, but you should use whatever oil you like.

RAI MASALA

MAKES ABOUT 5 TABLESPOONS

This is a simple roasted spice mixture that I use when making certain meat and vegetable dishes, such as the Pork (or Lamb) Kabobs (page 113).

2 tablespoons whole coriander seeds

2 teaspoons whole cumin seeds

1 teaspoon whole fenugreek seeds

1 teaspoon whole black or brown mustard seeds

5 whole cloves

1–2 dried hot red chilies

Set a small cast-iron or other heavy frying pan on medium-high heat. When hot, scatter in all the spices. Stir and roast until spices just begin to darken and emit a roasted aroma. This takes just a few minutes. Empty the spices onto a sheet of paper towel and let them cool. Grind all the spices together in a clean coffee grinder or spice grinder. Store in a tightly closed jar, away from sunlight. This mixture should be good for at least two months, although its aroma will decrease as time passes.

TAMARIND PASTE

Tamarind is the bean-like fruit of a tall shade tree. As tamarinds ripen, their sour green flesh turns a chocolate color. It remains sour, but picks up a hint of sweetness. For commercial purposes, tamarinds are peeled, seeded, and partly dried, and then compacted into rectangular blocks. These blocks need to be broken up and soaked in water. Then the pulp can be pushed through a strainer. This is tamarind paste.

To make your own tamarind paste: Break off ½ pound from a brick of tamarind and tear into small pieces. Put into a small nonmetallic pot and cover with 1 cup very hot water and set aside for 3 hours or overnight. (You could achieve the same result by simmering the tamarind for 10 minutes or by microwaving it for 3–5 minutes.) Set a sieve over a nonmetallic bowl and empty the tamarind and its soaking liquid into it. Push down on the tamarind with your fingers or the back of a wooden spoon to extract as much pulp as you can. Put whatever tamarind remains in the sieve back into the soaking bowl. Add ½ cup hot water to it and mash a bit more. Return it to the sieve and extract as much pulp as you can. Some of this pulp will be clinging to the underside of the sieve. Do not fail to retrieve it.

This quantity will make about 12 fluid ounces of thick paste. Whatever paste is left over may either be put into the refrigerator (where it will keep for 2–3 weeks) or frozen. It freezes well.

These days you can buy and use a readymade tamarind paste from Indian grocers. Make sure that it is not tamarind concentrate, which is dark and syrupy.

Lemon juice may be used as a substitute for tamarind paste.

TARKA (POPPING SPICES IN HOT OIL)

The "tarka" technique, known by many other names, such as "baghaar," "chownk," or "seasoning in oil," is quite unique to India, although simple versions of it are known in Italy, Spain, Cyprus, and even China. First, the oil has to be very hot. Then spices such as mustard seeds or cumin seeds—or just dried hot red chilies—are dropped into it. They pop and sizzle. Their whole character changes in an instant. They get much more intense. Their flavors change. Then, either this flavored oil with the seasonings in it is poured over cooked foods or foods are added to the oil and cooked in it. Since four or five spices can go into a tarka, they are often added to the hot oil in a certain order so that those that burn easily, such as dried chilies, go in last. The flavor of each is imparted to the oil. In the case of chilies, the flavor comes only from the browned skin. Any food cooked in this oil picks up the heightened flavor of all the spices.

Doing a tarka takes just a few seconds, so it is important to have all spices ready and at hand. A tarka is sometimes done at the beginning of a recipe, sometimes at the end, or even at both the beginning and the end. Legumes, for example, are usually just boiled with a little turmeric. When they are soft, a tarka is prepared in a small skillet, perhaps with asafetida, whole cumin, and red chilies, and then the entire contents of the skillet—the hot oil and spices—is poured over the legumes. Then the lid is shut tight for a few minutes to trap the aromas. Or the flavorings can be stirred in later. They perk up the boiled legumes and bring them to life.

TOMATO PUREE
When a recipe calls for tomato puree, bottled strained tomatoes, bottled passata, and canned puree may also be used.

WHOLE SPICES
When large whole spices such as cloves, bay leaves, and cinnamon sticks are used in a dish, they are not meant to be eaten. Just put them to the side as you would bones.

Index

Page numbers in italics refer to illustrations.

Light Sauce with Potatoes and Cauliflower, Chicken Stewed in a, 90–1

Lobhia Aur Khumbi, 27

M

Mango Soup, Gujarati, 5–6, *7*

Marwari Style, Potatoes in a, 47–8

meat, xi, 97–114

    Beef Oxtail in a Bazaari North Indian Red Sauce, 105–6, *107*

    cooking in Instant Pot, xi

    Goat Curry, 108–9

    Ground Lamb with Peas, 98–9

    Indian-Chinese Pork Chops, *110,* 111–12

    Kerala Lamb Stew, *100,* 101–2

    Lamb Mulligatawny Soup, 8, *9,* 10

    Lamb Pilaf, 126–9

    Lamb with Spinach, 103

    Pork (or Lamb) Kabobs, 113–14

    Rajasthani Red Braised Lamb, 104

    See also beef; chicken; goat; lamb; pork; turkey

Milk, Kerala Shrimp with Coconut, 61–2

Mint, Yogurt with Cucumber and, 146

Mixed-Vegetable Korma, South Indian, 51, *52, 53*

Mulligatawny Soup, Lamb or Chicken, 8, *9, 10*

Mung Dal, Rice, and Cabbage Soup, 11–12

Mung Dal, Simple, 17

Mung Dal with Spinach, 18, *19*

Murgh Makkhani, 80, 81–3

Musalmani Masoor, 28

mushroom:

    Black-Eyed Peas with Mushrooms, 27

    Southern-Style Mushrooms in a Creamy Coconut Style, *44, 45–6*

Muslim Style, Red Lentils Cooked in a, 28

mustard:

    Baby Arugula Salad with Mustard Oil, 136

    Salmon in a Bengali Mustard Sauce, 68–9

    Shrimp Steamed with Mustard, 60

My Garam Masala, 153–4

My Mother's Red Lentil Soup, 4

N

Noodles, Rice, 149

North Indian Red Sauce, Beef Oxtail in a Bazaari, 105–6, *107*

O

oil, 154

    Baby Arugula Salad with Mustard Oil, 136

    tarka (popping spices in hot oil), 156–7

onion:

    Cucumber, Onion, and Tomato Salad, 137

    Onion-Tomato Salad, 138

    Yogurt with Cucumbers, Tomatoes, and Onions, 147

Onion-Tomato Salad, 138

Oxtail in a Bazaari North Indian Red
  Sauce, Beef, 105–6, *107*

tomato (continued):

Eggs in a Tomato-Tamarind Hyderabadi
Sauce, 75–6, 77

Fresh Tomato Chutney, *140, 141*

Onion-Tomato Salad, 138

puree, 157

Quinoa with Tomatoes, 130, *131*

South Indian Mixed-Vegetable Korma,
51, *52, 53*

Squid in a Tomato-Chili Sauce, 70, *71*

Yogurt with Cucumbers, Tomatoes, and
Onions, 147

Turkey with Potatoes, Ground, 78–9

V

vegetables, 33–53

Beets in a Delhi-Style Tomato Sauce,
34, 35

Carrots and Peas with Sesame Seeds, 38

Cauliflower with Cilantro and Ginger,
40, 41, 42

Green Beans Stir-Fried in a South Indian
Style, *36, 37*

Kale Cooked in a Kashmiri Style, 43

Potatoes in a Marwari Style, 47–8

Southern-Style Mushrooms in a Creamy
Coconut Sauce, *44,* 45–6

South Indian Mixed-Vegetable Korma,
51, *52, 53*

Spicy Fat French Fries, 49–50

Sweet, Hot, and Sour Eggplants, 39

See also salads; *specific vegetables*

W

whole spices, 157

Y

Yakhni Pullao, 126–9

yogurt:

Chicken in a Yogurt Sauce, 87–8, *89*

Cold Yogurt Soup with Chickpeas,
Cucumbers, and Tomatoes, 2

Yogurt and Apple Raita, *144,* 145

Yogurt with Carrots and Raisins, 143

Yogurt with Cucumbers, Tomatoes, and
Onions, 147

Yogurt with Cucumbers and
Mint, 146

Yogurt and Apple Raita, *144, 145*

Yogurt with Carrots and Raisins, 143

Yogurt with Cucumber and Mint, 146

Yogurt with Cucumbers, Tomatoes, and
Onions, 147

Z

Zaafraan Uar Kishmish Ka Pullao, 123,
124, 125

Zucchini, Brown Lentils with, 29

A NOTE ABOUT THE AUTHOR

Madhur Jaffrey is the author of many previous cookbooks, seven of which have won James Beard Awards. Her first cookbook, *An Invitation to Indian Cooking*, has been inducted into the James Beard Hall of Fame, and she has been named to the Who's Who of Food and Beverage in America by the James Beard Foundation.

Jaffrey is an award-winning actress, having won the Silver Bear for Best Actress at the Berlin International Festival for the Merchant Ivory film *Shakespeare Wallah*. Her theater appearances include *Bombay Dreams* on Broadway and *Two Rooms* at the Signature Theater Company. She has many motion pictures to her credit, including *Prime* with Meryl Streep and *A Late Quartet* with Philip Seymour Hoffman. She was named a Commander of the Order of the British Empire by Queen Elizabeth II for her acting and her influence on the world of food. Miss Jaffrey has also appeared frequently on British and American television. Currently, she can be seen on NBC in the comedy series *I Feel Bad*.

A NOTE ON THE TYPE

This book was set in Scala, a typeface designed by the Dutch designer Martin Majoor (b. 1960) in 1988 and released by the FontFont foundry in 1990. While designed as a fully modern family of fonts containing both a serif and a sans serif alphabet, Scala retains many refinements normally associated with traditional fonts.

Composed by North Market Street Graphics,
Lancaster, Pennsylvania

Printed and bound by Friesen,
Canada

Designed by Soonyoung Kwon